MEDIA MADNESS

To my friend Brian Blank
with best wishes,
Jim Bowman
EPPC
February 28, 2008

Media Madness

The Corruption of Our Political Culture

JAMES BOWMAN

BRIEF ENCOUNTERS

Encounter Books · New York · London

Copyright © 2008 by James Bowman

First edition published in 2006 by Encounter Books, an activity of Encounter for Culture and Education, Inc., a nonprofit, tax exempt corporation.

Encounter Books website address: *www.encounterbooks.com*

Manufactured in the United States and printed on acid-free paper. The paper used in this publication meets the minimum requirements of ANSI/NISO Z39.48–1992 (R 1997) (Permanence of Paper).

FIRST EDITION

LIBRARY OF CONGRESS CATALOGING-IN-PUBLICATION DATA

Bowman, James, 1948–
Media madness : and the corruption of our political culture / James Bowman. — 1st ed.
   p.   cm. — (Brief encounters)
Includes bibliographical references and index.
ISBN-13: 978-1-59403-212-7 (hardcover : alk. paper)
ISBN-10: 1-59403-212-2 (hardcover : alk. paper) 1. Mass media—United States.   2. Mass media—Objectivity—United States.
3. Journalism—Objectivity—United States.   4. Journalism—Political aspects—United States.   5. United States—Politics and government—2001–   I. Title.
P92.U5B66 2008
302.230973 —dc22
2007041153

10 9 8 7 6 5 4 3 2 1

Contents

Dedicated to the memory of my mother,
Ruth Benscoter Bowman

Introduction: Ideology, Honor and the Media

"Is the Pope Catholic?"

That used to be the way people greeted a piece of news that wasn't news at all. Well now, apparently, the pope's being Catholic is news again. In July 2007, the Associated Press, Reuters, *The Washington Post*, *The Times* of London, and other papers informed us that, as *The Times* put it: "If it isn't Roman Catholic then it's not a proper church, Pope tells Christians."[1] Had the editors of *The Times* really been under the impression that the pope believed the church of which he is the head was just one of many "proper" churches? Had they been surprised to hear that the Bishop of Rome believed that the Roman Church was the one true church? I doubt it—though nowadays you never know. What made this news was that, in saying so, His Holiness could be deemed to have been insensitive and offensive to non-Catholics. True, the few whose reactions were recorded were disappointingly low on outrage, but it was a given that their feelings must have been hurt, their self-esteem wounded. A respected spiritual leader whose religion requires him to love his enemies—and therefore, presumably, to be nice to them—had shown disrespect towards those who think that their churches are also proper churches.

Probably there were not many people who read the news of the pope's Catholicism and thought that the gimlet-eyed media had uncovered yet another block-busting scandal about the great and the powerful—though there must have been at least a few at *The Times* and elsewhere who were prepared to hope that, for a day or two at least, it could be sold as a sort of mini-scandal. Their unspoken reasoning must have gone something like this: not only was the pope a hypocrite for disrespecting and not being nice to some of his fellow Christians, but in claiming for his own beliefs a privileged position he was guilty of the first and greatest sin against the creed of the media, which is arrogance. Does he think he's better than we are? That's just your opinion, man. What makes you think you're infallible?

Arrogance would have been a better way to characterize the attitude of the media themselves. Not the supposed arrogance of merely believing what one believes but the real arrogance of assuming that no other belief is possible without the assumption of the believer's lunacy, imbecility, viciousness, corruption, or some combination of all four to explain it. This assumption is the product of what I call *media madness*, though of course it is not limited to the media. In fact, its spread outside the media to other social elites, and especially to our political and intellectual classes, is what has inspired me to write this book. Media madness has come into existence, as I hope to show, through the peculiar conditions that prevailed during the century or so of the mass media's greatest power and influence, and through the gradual elimination of any authority in church or state or even in scientific or intellectual life to which the media, or those who think as the media have taught us to think, might defer.

Let me stress that media madness is not a form of mental illness or any sort of clinical condition. The psychoanalyzing of those with whom we disagree and the diagnosis in them of incipient or actual insanity is a characteristic of media madness itself and not of its description. The state of mind it thus describes is rather to be understood as a sort of *folie de grandeur* on the part of ordinary but self-important people who haven't the excuse of insanity for their lack of humility and a sense of proportion. It lives and thrives among those who are perfectly healthy but whose culture has provided them with no natural check on their confidence in their own intellectual powers at the same time that it has fostered in them a powerful need for the status nowadays to be claimed by the exercise of such powers.

Media madness is a product of the same commercial, sociological, and intellectual conditions that brought the mass media into existence and to the peak of their influence. These conditions include the pretense of "objectivity," the subject of Chapter One, and the cult of feelings, to which I turn in Chapter Two. In Chapter Three, I will try to explain how tolerance for the sort of sensationalism and hyperbole used to sell more papers or television advertising warps the media's sense of reality, and, in Chapter Four, how pandering to the meritocracy's overvaluation of intelligence does the same. In Chapter Five, I will look into the influence of the therapeutic culture on the media, and how it flatters their sense of their own superiority, especially to those who are engaged in the conflicts that still make up so much of what we think of as news. Finally, in Chapter Six, I show how the media's celebrity-worship and belief in their own non-partisanship encourage and are encouraged by the growing tendency in public life to turn political into moral matters and so to remove them from the realm of legitimate debate.

This moralization of political life—and its contribution to the "polarization" and "incivility" that, when it suits them to do so, the media complain most loudly about—now looks like becoming the most lasting legacy of the media culture. The style of thought and the set of presumptions about the world which have been created by the material circumstances of the mass media have spread well beyond them. Now, even among ordinary educated people that style and those presumptions have become commonplace, with serious consequences for our national conversation about public matters. What made me want to write this book was not a wish to attack the media, or to go back over the old ground of media "bias," but rather to note and deplore the way in which media madness has produced a breakdown of the common political language and an impoverishment of the ability of the two sides in a democratic debate to talk to each other.

THE END OF THE MEDIA
AS WE KNOW THEM

As I have been writing *Media Madness*, I have been able to watch the construction on Pennsylvania Avenue in Washington, D.C., of a $435-million-dollar monument to the media's self-importance called "The Newseum." Situated between the Capitol and the White House and obviously intended to have something of their monumental character, the museum with the name of a punning headline is due to open in 2008 and is being financed by the Freedom Forum, a foundation set up by Al Neuharth of Gannett and *USA Today*. As its predecessor in Arlington, Virginia, did in the 1990s, it will tell the heroic story of the media as the media see it. It is a story most of which dates no further back than the 1960s, when media triumphalism claims to have been instrumental in the success of the Civil Rights movement, and subsequently in the failure (they don't call it that) of the Vietnam War and the destruction of the presidency of Richard Nixon. These are the founding legends of the contemporary media culture and, along with the First Amendment—a 74-foot-high marble engraving of which already adorns the building's façade—the basis for the media's belief in their quasi-constitutional role in the governance of the country.

Yet within a very few years of the Newseum's opening, it is likely to be seen as commemorating not these journalistic landmarks so much as a way of life that belonged to the twentieth century, not the twenty-first. For the media, as we understand that term, are finished. Or should that be "is finished"? For the fifteen years that I have been writing about the media, and during the much briefer span of the writing of this book, I have had always to bear in mind that the word is a Latin plural and therefore should be accompanied by a plural verb. Why is that so hard to remember? I am constantly catching myself using the singular verb. (Perhaps, the odd singular might even have crept through the rigorous screening this book has received to survive in the text you hold in your hands. If so I apologize for the error.)

But the reason for it is that the media as we have experienced them for decades past have almost invariably seemed like one thing rather than many things. That is what is finished. Within the next ten or twenty years it will almost certainly be the case for all of us, as it already is for the mostly younger people who get their news from the Internet, cable television, and radio talk shows, that the media will again seem like many things rather than one thing. On the whole, this is a development warmly to be welcomed. Like the collapse of communist bureaucracies in many of the lands where Marxist-Leninist orthodoxy once held sway, the wasting away of the stiflingly monolithic media—the period of whose heyday so nearly corresponded with that of the Soviet Union—means freedom for all from the tyranny of an ideology whose death grip on power bore no relation either to its current acceptance or its intellectual coherence.

The media that have come into existence for the purpose of shaping or exploiting mass opinion will have to reinvent themselves—and, indeed, are already beginning to reinvent themselves—so as to cater to an almost infinite number of niche audiences instead. Yet at the point where people in their various niches have to talk to each other—the point, that is, where public and political life must always be lived— the language of our national conversation is to an unfortunate extent still based on the legacy of the old mass media, whose influence is thus spreading—to politicians and even to ordinary people—even as their power is diminishing. The fragmentation of the media means, among other and mostly good things, that the tendency which the media have created of each side in the public debate only to talk to the like-minded and not to each other will probably even increase.

The only thing that might stop this from happening is that we will come to recognize media madness when we see it and begin to re-assert the need for real debate in the place of that which now mostly goes under that name but whose routine accusations of bad faith, corruption, or mental illness are really the death of rational discourse. Not everyone in the media engages in this kind of destructive dialogue, but it was largely a media-derived impulse which brought it into being and has continued to make it as widespread as it now is. In an age in which, as the lawyer Scott Gant says, "We're all Journalists Now,"[2] it seems to me no longer necessary that so many of us should write and think and talk like journalists.

In my last book, *Honor: A History*,[3] I characterized the last three decades as "post-honor society"—a phrase not invented by me but by an outsider to that society, the anthropologist Akbar S. Ahmed, who implicitly compared our society to the honor culture of the Islamic world. The mind of the media and therefore the media madness that it has given rise to has also been formed by this post-honor society. In the honor cultures of the non-Western world, as in our own culture up until eighty or ninety years ago, reputation has an importance that it is now difficult for us to imagine. People in such cultures live their lives according to social expectations and feel no shame about it. On the contrary, shame is reserved for those who insist on going their own way without regard to social expectation. Quite often, as in the case of "honor killings," that shame has lethal consequences for those who live according to its rules.

In a world where reputation is more important than life itself, it will be readily understood, the place for such professional disturbers and debunkers of reputation as journalists must be both limited and dangerous, as in fact we see it is in the honor culture of Islam with which we increasingly find ourselves living at uncomfortably close quarters. Just ask Salman Rushdie or Theo van Gogh or Ayaan Hirsi Ali.

Few in the West would wish for the cruel discipline imposed on the media by such an honor culture, but the destruction of our more benign and tolerant version of an honor culture has allowed media madness to grow and spread like some pest whose natural predators have been eliminated. We can only hope that that growth will ultimately be checked, if not by a revival of the Western honor culture, then by the ridicule that will eventually greet such absurdities as trying to raise a scandal over the pope's being Catholic. If this book is successful in holding up similar examples of media madness to such ridicule, it will have accomplished its purpose.

1 | The Illusions of "Objectivity" and "Professionalism"

IN CAUTIOUSLY WELCOMING the departure from traditional standards of "objectivity" in the new media—especially by cable news "personalities" like Lou Dobbs, Bill O'Reilly, and Anderson Cooper—Michael Kinsley in 2006 wrote:

> Opinion journalism can be more honest than objective-style journalism, because it doesn't have to hide its point of view. All observations are subjective. Writers freed of artificial objectivity can try to determine the whole truth about their subject and then tell it whole to the world. Their "objective" counterparts have to sort their subjective observations into two arbitrary piles: truths that are objective as well, and truths that are just an opinion. That second pile of truths cannot be published, except perhaps as a quote from someone else. Without the pretense of objectivity, the fundamental journalist's obligation of factual accuracy would remain. Opinion journalism brings new ethical obligations as well. These can be summarized in two words: intellectual honesty.[1]

New ethical obligations? This unconsciously revealing phrase suggests that Mr. Kinsley is very well aware of the dishonesty that prevails under the reign of "objectivity." He himself has just admitted it by pointing to the fact that, unlike "objective-style journalism"—compare: "leather-style upholstery"—opinion journalism "doesn't *have* to hide its point of view." But he doesn't mention directly the difficulties and dishonesties occasioned by the fact that the media behave as if they thought that hiding one's point of view were the same as not having a point of view, or not being affected and influenced by one. And everyone knows that this is not the case.

Our way of looking at things determines what we see. In setting out to explain the media's way of looking at the world, I first have to take account of the curious fact that the media almost invariably deny that they have a way of looking at the world. For if the routine journalistic claim to "objectivity" means anything, it must mean this. Merely being a journalist is implicitly supposed to endow one with the capacity to transcend one's point of view, and the cachet of objectivity even lends its authority at one remove to avowed opinion writers who look down their noses at the likes of Rush Limbaugh because his opinions do not issue from an *echt* journalist like themselves.

THE COMMERCIAL IMPORTANCE OF CLINGING TO MYTHS OF "OBJECTIVITY" AND "PROFESSIONALISM"

Journalists seem not to know that objectivity is a long-exploded myth. Epistemology has been pretty emphatic for the past two centuries that no one can be truly objective. The so-called "Kantian revolution" in philosophy—against the old, theologically-based certainties and the Newtonian rationalism that had followed them in making universal truth-claims—insisted that we all must have a point of view of the world, if only because we can't see all of it at once. That point of view is not separable from what we see and, therefore, what we think and say about it. There is no shame in not being objective, since nobody can be. But there is, or ought to be, shame in obstinately denying what must be true, or affirming what must be false, as so many in the media do with respect to their own objectivity.

This is what leads to media madness. Those afflicted by it are Kantian counterrevolutionaries—though of course they never attempt to make any kind of philosophical argument on behalf of objectivity. Instead, they are content to rely on a sort of gentleman's agreement among themselves to ignore the whole question—except to deny it furiously when someone accuses them of bias—and, with it, the intellectual discredit objectivity has suffered over the last two hundred years. This has now become the skeleton in the journalistic family closet of which no one must ever speak. Fortunately for those who would keep it hidden, the popular prejudice in favor of objectivity and the certainties of a rationally observable universe has remained largely untroubled by Kant, Einstein, or any more up-to-date criticisms—enough so as to provide the media a necessary cover for the myth not only of their own objectivity but also of the very existence of such a thing.

Unlike objectivity, professionalism really does exist, though it is now used loosely by journalists as by others to mean nothing more than a sort of business etiquette. Journalists may be as "professional" in their behavior as real estate agents or dental hygienists, but that doesn't make journalism a profession any more than selling houses or cleaning teeth are professions. Journalism is a trade whose basic intellectual tools can be swiftly acquired and are best learned through apprenticeship, yet grandiose schools of journalism have been set up at universities throughout the country in order to create the impression that being a news-hound is like being a lawyer or a doctor. It isn't. Unlike law or medicine, journalism does not require the mastery of any body of scholarship or knowledge. The relevant knowledge for a reporter is not of journalistic technique and precedent but of whatever it is that he's reporting on—business, sports, politics, the arts, fashion.[2] If instead of learning these things in preparation for his calling he seeks a "professional" qual-ification, it is because the existence of "J-Schools" alongside schools of law or medicine is meant to suggest that you can learn the mysteries of journalism, including objectivity, as you learn those of real professions.

Both these myths, of objectivity and professionalism, came into existence for commercial reasons and, as the eco-nomics of the news business becomes more and more pre-carious, the dinosaurs of the now-declining era of the mass media cling ever more tightly to them. For the economic viability of those media depends on the plausibility with which they are able to claim a privileged position with respect to information management. The twin pretenses of objec-tivity and professionalism are what allow the journalist to claim that privilege, at least so long as they are believed. The marketability of the perishable information he has to offer for sale depends to an extent that no one has ever been able

to measure on a notional objectivity and professionalism—
which is why his commitment to those qualities must be
defended so fiercely.

Since the advent of the Internet, the cultural privilege
claimed by the media has been under threat as never before.
"The Internet today is like the American West in the 1880s.
It's wild, it's crazy and everybody's got a gun.... There are
no rules yet." Thus Thomas Kunkel, dean of the University
of Maryland's journalism school in a worried and fretful
article on the front of the business section of *The Washington Post* in January, 2007.[3] Both Dean Kunkel and the *Post*'s
reporter, Alan Sipress, were anxious about the granting of
press credentials to bloggers for the trial of Vice President
Cheney's former chief of staff, I. Lewis "Scooter" Libby, on
charges of perjury and obstruction of justice. You can
understand why they and others in the media establishment
might think of bloggers as a species of stagecoach robbers,
come to take the bread out of their mouths. Who's going to
pay *them* to collect and analyze information, or to prepare
the "professionals" who perform those tasks on our behalf,
when there's a whole army of amateurs prepared to do it for
nothing?

The article included a classic newspaper bar graph titled
"Blogging Without Journalistic Standards" in which we were
told that significant percentages of bloggers, according to a
survey by the Pew Internet and American Life Project, "don't
abide by some common journalistic practices." For instance,
the survey asked a sampling of the bloggers if they "spend
extra time verifying facts" or "quote other people directly"
or "get permission to post copyrighted material" or "include

links to original source material" or "post corrections." Between 41 and 61 percent answered "Never" or "Hardly ever" to these questions. There was no comparable survey of professional journalists, but I think we can assume that they would have reported themselves as being *much* more observant of such "common journalistic practices."

THE JOURNALISTIC MAINSTREAM IS DRYING UP...

Such articles are written with an uneasy sense that professional journalism itself is changing. A few days before this piece ran in the *Post*, *The Wall Street Journal* had announced with some fanfare a number of changes—including a reduction in size—designed to take account of the way that most people now get their news. "Your print *Journal* will now focus even more on 'what the news means,'" wrote the publisher, L. Gordon Crovitz, "beyond simply what happened yesterday"—which he could assume that most people would already know. "These innovations are meant to establish the *Journal* as the first newspaper rethought for how readers increasingly now get their news, often in real time, from many sources, all day long."[4] Not that he was abandoning any attempt at "real time" monitoring of the news. Far from it! "*The Wall Street Journal* Online is the place to go for 'what's happening right now' news on the Web, through mobile devices and across online video and audio," he wrote, and he went on to detail the new range of online features available to those who subscribe, for the *Journal*, unlike almost every other newspaper in the world, is able to charge for its online services.[5]

The *Journal*'s ability to charge puts it in a position in relation to potential competitors analogous to the relationship between the major metropolitan dailies and the free papers or "shoppers" that have sprung up everywhere in the last twenty years or so—and that, collectively, are a kind of *memento mori*, representing the future of the major metropolitan dailies. Most of the once-proud newspapers of America already find themselves online in the position of the shoppers—that is, giving away their hard-won "content" for free in the hopes of winning a large enough audience to attract advertisers in numbers sufficient to cover their costs and make a profit. In this situation it must become ever more important for traditional newspapers, crammed full of "professional" journalists with an understandable pride in their craft and an understandable anxiety for their pretty well-remunerated livelihoods to do all that they can to accentuate their differences from the bloggers and others who are also providing free content.

Of all the differences that the media can point to as offering added value to ordinary Internet surfers, objectivity—or at least the illusion of objectivity—must stand at the head of the list. It is the guarantor of their authority, and authority is really the only thing that the commercial media have to bring to market which gives them an advantage over the new media and the blogosphere that are otherwise such terrifying threats to them. Information can be had anywhere on the Internet for nothing. It's the authority with which information can be certified as accurate that only makes it worth charging for. What gives the media's information that notional authority is partly the fact that they have paid for it themselves in the form of the immense capital costs—

high-priced reporters, expensive equipment and the crews to man it, foreign bureaux, etc.—which they incur to put out a newspaper or mount a television or radio news operation. But mostly it is their reputation for objectivity. Hence the violent hatred of the media-mad towards those, like Bernard Goldberg in his 2001 book *Bias*,[6] who dare to call that objectivity into question.

Yet in another way, Mr. Goldberg and his kind must come as a relief to the media, since fighting back against the individual charges of bias serves as a distraction from the structural bias that remains largely unremarked on. Even among bloggers, it is still possible to pass a negative comment on something by questioning its objectivity, although the famously pajama-clad commentators who manage their own blogs really owe their existence to its denial as much as the mainstream media do to its affirmation. It is their more often unashamed *lack* of objectivity which is precisely their charm for most of those who are seeking them out in increasing numbers. Blog-consumers, like listeners to talk radio and cable news, look to their sources of information for ideological sympathy. In a world where it is ever more difficult to know whom to trust, we are much readier to trust those who share our prejudices and worldviews than those who do not.[7]

... BUT PEOPLE STILL REMEMBER IT FONDLY

To me, the remarkable thing is how much trust there still is in the "mainstream" media—that is, the major television networks, metropolitan dailies, and newsmagazines—and their claims to be without bias. In an opinion poll taken by the Pew Research Center in 2004, for example, only 42 percent of Republicans said that they thought the media were biased towards the Democrats.[8] That touching degree of public trust in their claims to objectivity is money in the bank to the media, though independent surveys[9] as well as casual observation support the claim by Thomas Edsall, a former *Washington Post* reporter and a liberal Democrat,[10] that the political reporters he knew were Democratic in a ratio of somewhere between 15 and 25 to 1 over Republican. A 2007 survey by Bill Dedman of MSNBC showed that of 143 journalists who had made political contributions from 2004 onwards, 125 of them gave to the Democrats and only 16 to the Republicans (two gave to both parties).[11] That's only a little under eight-to-one, but it's still pretty lopsided. It therefore seems probable that the 29 percent of Democrats in the Pew poll who thought the media biased to the Republicans were really reacting to the fact that the media were not showing their bias *enough* but, by keeping it under wraps as much as they still did, were letting President Bush off too lightly.[12] Of course such figures are always cited by the media as if the fact that they are accused of bias by both partisan sides must mean that they're *not* biased, rather than, as anyone aggregating the totals would have to join the Kantians in saying, that they *are* biased. Eric Alterman is right in saying that the "liberal" media are more conservative than he, but so are many of his counterparts on the right in saying that the media are still *much* more liberal than they are.

Where, as in Mr. Edsall's case, bias is openly admitted, it is usually not taken very seriously. Thus Gene Weingarten recently wrote in *The Washington Post Magazine* that "We in the media are sometimes accused of letting liberal bias subtly slip into our writing and reporting. That accusation is calumny. We are dispassionate observers and seekers of truth. All we do is ask questions. Today's question: Is George W. Bush the worst president in American history?" That's a joke, you see. So is Andy Rooney's saying on CBS's "60 Minutes" after the 2004 election: "I know a lot of you believe that most people in the news business are liberal. Let me tell you, I know a lot of them, and they were almost evenly divided this time. Half of them liked Senator Kerry; the other half hated President Bush."[13] CBS, you may remember, was the network where hatred of the president had seemed to predominate when Dan Rather attempted in the middle of the 2004 election campaign to raise a scandal about him based on forged documents. And yet this confirmation of anti-Bush bias could still be treated—as it was clearly expected to be treated—as a mere pleasantry. There seems to be at work here an acknowledgment that the secret is out but also an assumption that, if you can make a joke about it, it must be all right. At one level, Messrs. Weingarten and Rooney can be construed as saying that we're so sure this *isn't* true that we can joke about it while at another level, they're saying, we're so sure it *is* true that we can joke about it. Either way, the bias that is acknowledged and laughed about must be supposed to have no relation to the bias that is routinely and furiously denied when the likes of Bernard Goldberg point it out.

OBJECTIVITY VS. FAIRNESS

Objectivity is the established church of the media. You don't have to be a regular worshiper; you may even attend another church unofficially. But you do have to genuflect to it on all official occasions, since it is what stamps your credentials as a journalist. Without that certificate, you're just a glorified blogger. Claims to objectivity also have a side benefit, as the media have come to see it, in largely eliminating the need for fairness. For objectivity and fairness are antithetical terms.[14] If you are truly objective, what need do you have to be fair? You speak, as it were, from no point of view—or all points of view at once, which comes to the same thing. In other words, you speak with the voice of God. To believe this is the very essence of media madness, and it is to eliminate the need for fairness. It is only when bias is acknowledged that fairness becomes a consideration. In an artificially limited arena such as a basketball court or a football field, where it is at least closer to being possible for someone to see everything, the idea of objectivity makes a certain amount of sense, and it is what we expect of referees and umpires. There we may use "fair" and "fairness" in the negative—that's unfair—to mean a falling away from the standard of objectivity, but what we really mean is that the ump is biased towards one side or against another.

It is normally the other team and not the referee that we expect to "play fair"—by which we mean not only according to the rules but also with a certain standard of honor, decorum, and gentlemanliness in those areas where the rules do not operate or are vague, say in the case of taunting or insulting one's opponent. Similarly, in matters of political controversy and partisanship, if I admit that I take a particular point of view, that of one party or another, then I automatically create a *prima facie* obligation for myself to be fair to the other party and to other points of view in general—by, for example, not misrepresenting them in order to make my own polemical work easier, or not questioning their good faith. Under the regime of "objectivity" and the media madness it generates, both of these kinds of unfairness have become routine in American public life. To suppose that there is an "objective" or a nonpartisan point of view of any conflict is to render the whole question of fairness moot. We may choose to be kind, but we have no need to be fair to those who are simply in error.

To the extent that this is the media's point of view—to insist that they haven't got one—there exists a community of interest in the media, binding together those of otherwise disparate views. Gradually this community of interest has become far more influential in shaping the media consensus and driving it in the direction of media madness than their common political persuasion in favor of Democrats and "progressives"—important as that is at election time. The media continue, for the most part, to have a certain delicacy about being explicit in the pointing out of what, by their lights, is error, but neither do they see any need for fairness or generosity towards it so long as they remain persuaded of the "objectivity" of the point of view from which it is identified. The more tenaciously someone clings to the Myth of Objectivity, therefore, the more likely he is to use it to justify acts of unfairness.

Objective Means Liberal?

A perfect illustration may be found in the case mentioned above, in which Dan Rather could hardly have been unaware of the likely electoral benefit to Senator Kerry of aspersions cast on President Bush's military record, which turned out to be based on forged documents. It was a blogger who first called the world's attention to the proportional spacing used in the document on which Mr. Rather's report was based. Proportional spacing, routine on today's computer-based word-processing programs, was only available in 1973 on expensive type-setting machines such as the IBM Selectric, which were very far from being standard government issue to colonels in the Air National Guard. As the document's chain of custody was in any case non-existent—it was supposedly handed to Mr. Rather's source by someone he didn't know in a public place—the case was overwhelming for forgery, and yet both Dan Rather and the source continued to deny it, and deny it to this day, on the basis of the fact that those who exposed the forgery were "partisans."

The absurdity of Dan Rather's pretending, first, that this was a fact of the slightest relevance and, second, that he himself was *not* a partisan but something higher, purer, and better and so unassailable by those grubby little souls who exist somewhere far beneath the Olympian heights on which he dwells was obvious to anyone not in thrall to the Myth of Objectivity, the sanctuary of which Mr. Rather was, in effect, claiming. Without the lingering strength among the public of that same myth as it survives in the polite fiction on which the network news itself is founded—namely that journalists who report the news are invariably nonpartisan—he could not have hoped to make without ridicule and obloquy the argument, which he has continued to make since, that the document was genuine and that he was, in any case, simply doing his "professional" duty in reporting what it said. On another occasion[15] he even attempted similarly to explain away his having given a speech at a Democratic fundraiser.

Invoke the magic of "objectivity" and even overt partisanship became partisanship no more.

All those things that the bloggers don't do—checking facts and quoting people, for instance—do not add up to objectivity or anything close to it, but the claims of professionalism on behalf of what remains, at best, a trade, is meant to make it seem as if they do. It is a kind of cloak of journalistic invisibility that anyone employed by a mainstream media outlet feels entitled to slip into whenever he is charged with bias or partisanship. Howard Kurtz, the media correspondent of *The Washington Post* recorded the reaction of John Harris, executive editor of *The Politico* and a former *Post* reporter, when a Bush administration official pointed out to him that one of his reporters on a story about the administration's anti-drug propaganda campaign had worked for an advocacy group for the legalization of marijuana. "There are lot of people at publications who have gone from advocacy jobs in a previous career to non-advocacy roles," Mr. Harris told Mr. Kurtz. "The story was motivated by journalistic interest, not his particular views on the subject." [16]

Here was a story that was critical of a government program towards which the author had himself publicly proclaimed his hostility by taking up an "advocacy job" and we were supposed to consider this a fact of no relevance? Such a preposterous notion could only have been advanced by someone who could be sure that, whoever else was drugged up, the media's watchdogs certainly were. Mr. Kurtz's column in the *Post* is, like the various "ombudsman" columns that have sprung like mushrooms in the newspapers of America, practically founded on the journalistic trick of citing allegations of bias or malfeasance, beating the columnar breast about it for a paragraph or two, asking if objectivity and professionalism can be preserved or reestablished, and concluding that—well, yes they can. Merely asking the question thus becomes a means of reinforcing the self-satisfaction that creates the bias in the first place while simultaneously implying that it doesn't exist, except in trivial ways or by inadvertently going "too far"—as in the BBC's recent admission that it had been too open and uncritical in its support of various celebrity Save the World projects.[17] It wasn't as if there could be much to be ashamed of in the media's tendency "to side with the powerless rather than the powerful," as Walter Cronkite once put it. "If that is what makes us liberals, so be it, just as long as in reporting the news we adhere to the first ideals of good journalism— that news reports must be fair, accurate and unbiased."[18] In other words, being a liberal in this self-congratulatory sense is apparently perfectly consistent with being objective and unbiased. After all, as Mr. Cronkite went on to point out, one of the Random House dictionary's synonyms for "liberal" is "unprejudiced."[19]

"Objectivity" Produces Scandal Politics

The outrageousness of the pretense of objectivity is considerably increased by the obviousness of the media's partisanship in the last two American elections. Dan Rather's attempt to take down President Bush with a bogus scandal was too much even for CBS in 2004, and he lost his job on account of it. But if he was the most daring of the media partisans during that election campaign, he was very far from being the only one.[20] Although Mr. Rather's bogus scandal had the effect of snuffing it out, the effort to find something of discredit in President Bush's service record had been going on in the media all year long, and the alleged scandal had made the cover of *Newsweek* some months before. Yet no one appeared to notice any self-contradiction when the media, after trying for some weeks to ignore a similar rummage through Senator Kerry's service record by an organization called Swift Boat Veterans for Truth, branded that effort as illegitimate—indeed, outrageous.[21] And in 2006, *The Washington Post*—which proclaims itself "An Independent Newspaper" on its masthead—engaged in a blatant campaign of scandal-mongering against Republican candidates, especially Senator George Allen of Virginia.[22] Such examples would make a mockery of the media's claims to objectivity even if we did not already know that objectivity is impossible. But they could not have happened without the pretense of objectivity, one of whose consequences is to reduce all elections and, indeed, all politics to rival scandal-narratives.

So long as the media must pretend to be nonpartisan, their coverage will tend to avoid real political disagreements, which can often hardly be discussed without taking one side or the other, and focus instead on such nonpolitical but still serious matters as alleged faults of character, morality, or judgment. In the case of Senator Allen, the *Post* found ever more ingenious ways to insinuate that he was a racist without using the word and without breaking the pretense that it was only raising the curtain on legitimate matters of public interest which the candidate had, equally discreditably, wished to keep hidden. "It's not the crime but the cover-up," has become a media cliché in the years since Watergate, but now we see—as in the case of I. Lewis

"Scooter" Libby—there can be a cover-up even when there is no crime. That didn't stop the special prosecutor, Patrick Fitzgerald, from making the cover-up the crime, in the absence of any other. It was yet another indication of the extent to which the media's scandal-politics has now taken over for serious and substantive politics.

Even the wish of politicians or others to keep what would once have been thought of as legitimately private matters private has itself become a scandal—at least if the media are to be believed, as they almost invariably were in the case of Congressman Mark Foley in 2006. The congressman's sexual attraction to teenage boys and young men had, so far as anyone knew, never been acted upon and—at the time the scandal broke—was manifest only in an e-mailed request to a teenager for a photograph. Yet the Republican leadership in the House of Representatives was raked over the coals even in some of the so-called "conservative" media for not having been out ahead of *The Washington Post* in crying scandal against their colleague and political ally on the strength of no more evidence than that e-mail. Clearly, we live in an age of scandal, and the media like it that way. But increasingly we find that scandal is self-generating and crowds out more legitimate sorts of interest in public matters.[23]

In all the cases mentioned above, the media's strong commercial interests as well as their claims to objectivity lie with the promotion of scandal, or quasi-scandal, to the center of the political process. The resources of big media give them a big advantage over the small or amateur kind when it comes to "investigative reporting," so it follows that it is in their interest to make the investigative sort of reporting an ever more prominent part of their political coverage. Like the pretense of objectivity, the pretense that they are lifting the veil to show you the hidden things someone doesn't want you to know about is vital if their business is to survive the big shake-out created by the new media. Whether or not it is in their country's interest for politicians to know fewer and fewer ways of running for office without finding matter to demonstrate the unfitness of their opponents—not just to serve but even to hold their heads up in public—is not a question they can afford to entertain, let alone care about. Even when there is no scandal involved, the media's interest in suggesting that they can take you behind the scenes to show you the hidden emotional origins of public and political behavior continually distorts their and our perceptions of the world—as we shall see in the next chapter.

2 | Taking Us Behind the Scenes: Feelings, Failings, and Foibles

THE HEADLINE IN *The Times* of London[1] read as follows: "I'm going to die, skydiver thought as he fell 15,000 ft ... into a bush." Now this was not what I would call news. What else would the skydiver think? What else would anyone think? Of course, the news was that the skydiver *didn't* die, but you had to go to the story to find that out. Yet somehow "Skydiver survives 15,000-foot fall"—both headlines assume the reader will guess that the "fall" was without a parachute—was thought of as less sexy, less alluring. Why? Because the consumers of news today have been taught by the media's example that feelings are much more important than events. In fact, events very often *are* feelings, or the expression of feelings, much more than they are anything else. Demonstrations, invariably staged for the benefit of the media, are so called because they are demonstrations of feeling, of passion, of indignation and anger. That's how they become news. Recognizing this, terrorists in Iraq and elsewhere commit their murders more for the sake of the media coverage they will generate than in the hope that they will accomplish any political ends themselves.

By convention, if not in reality, these murderous acts represent the spontaneous overflow of powerful feelings just as (more or less) peaceful demonstrations do among non-terrorists. And the strength of the feelings that the terrorists and the demonstrators are able to evince by their actions tends to be used, however irrationally, as an indicator of the rightness of the cause in which they are made manifest. There is no logic or consistency in feelings, no right or wrong. They simply are, and so, unlike thoughts, they can easily be reported without interfering with the pretense of objectivity—even when they are self-contradictory. As a recent *New York Times* headline put it: "Voters Excited Over '08 Campaign; Tired of It, Too."[2]

THE CULTURE OF EMOTIONALISM

This fascination with feeling is part of what the British sociologist Frank Furedi calls "the culture of emotionalism," and it arises out of the increasingly general acceptance of a set of therapeutic maxims about the world that put feelings at the center of our attention.[3] But if the culture is already predisposed to think in terms of emotions, the tendency is also helped along by another of the media's commercial interests. Just as a belief in objectivity helps them to sell their information product, so does a belief that they are in a position to mine the "real" feelings that lie beneath the increasingly bland and featureless landscape of public utterance. Ideally, these feelings will be discreditable, even scandalous, since nothing that the media has to sell sells better than scandal, but even ordinary feelings brought out from semi-obscurity and held up for our inspection provide the media with the interpretive, mediating role that is their bread and butter.

The most interesting feeling of all for writers on politics, as on other subjects, is anger. President Bush is angry with the terrorists, the Democrats are angry with President

Bush, the anti-war left is angry with the Democrats, and the few remaining Bush supporters are angry with the anti-war left. These various angers can be swapped around almost at will, each being seen as an explanation for another, as well as for the things that the angry person does. "Why do they hate us?" *Newsweek* famously asked in the wake of the 9/11 terror-attacks. But maybe this was the wrong question. Maybe they didn't hate us; maybe they just wanted to kill us. But to the media-mad, happily rooting around for the hidden emotional origins of behavior, this was an almost unthinkable thought.

By now, this obsession with feelings as the touchstone of authenticity has come to mean that democratic politicians are finding that they, too, must play the game of the demonstrators and the terrorists by advertising their feelings of anger or compassion in a given instance where one or another or both are required.[4] Because feelings have traditionally been private and therefore hidden away from the public gaze—as, of course, social convention demands that they still mostly are for those of us who live out of the public eye—the media's promise to reveal them appeals to a prurient impulse in the public. Their ability to represent themselves as taking us behind the scenes in order to reveal the private emotions that are supposed to be the "real" causes of public events is an obvious selling point to those who might otherwise be reluctant to lay out hard cash for the services they provide—and especially to the large number of those who are disposed to believe that the most interesting things about public events are the private side of them.

Moreover, if public men and women want for whatever reason to keep certain thoughts and feelings out of the public view, that in itself is reason enough for many, schooled in the cynicism of the media, to see the hidden matters as more "real" than the public ones. Yet these supposedly real feelings cannot be that, whatever else they are. Just as there is no such thing as true objectivity, so there is no such thing as a true feeling in public, since the act of making it public has a distorting effect. Like elementary particles, feelings can only be observed once they have ceased to be whatever it was they were before observation's spotlight shone upon them. The public face of a public figure may or may not be the truth about him, and the process of inference from his actions as to whether or not it is the truth is or ought to be a proper journalistic exercise. But the media-mad, intoxicated with their belief in the authenticity of feelings, are terribly credulous in assuming that the glimpses of a public person's private life provided by his feelings, or those of his acquaintances, colleagues, or subordinates, is mere "reality."

POLITICS AND CELEBRITY

The perfection of the passio-centric universe is our celebrity culture, so it is not surprising that the media's coverage of everything more and more tends to resemble their coverage of celebrities. Celebrities have always staked their claim on our attention by demonstrating authentic feeling—or something that can pass for it. Fame, on this view, is an intimidating and repellent thing to ordinary, unfamous people without this reassurance by the "stars" that they are, as *Us Weekly* magazine puts it, "just like us." Back in the days of heroes, fame was thought to be the reward of the exceptional. But we have replaced heroes with celebrities and in doing so have let it be known that what we cared about was the unexceptional, the ordinary, what is routinely called the "human" side of these new paragons. They had to come down from Olympus and show us their feelings as the only acceptable justification for their distinction from the rest of us. I shall have more to say about celebrity and celebrities in Chapter Six,[5] but here we may notice that politicians used not to be celebrities, and the range of the emotions they were allowed to express was accordingly limited. They could express feelings associated with strength—feelings such as joy, confidence, or determination—but not feelings associated with weakness.

Even today, this is still true to some extent and is a holdover from an era in which we expected our leaders to be more like heroes than they were like movie stars. Jimmy Carter's "malaise" speech in the summer of 1979 was widely regarded as an expression of weakness and must have contributed to his being turned out of office a little over a year later. The word "malaise" was, as a matter of fact, not in the speech itself, but, right after the opening mention of its being the anniversary of his nomination by his party as its candidate for the presidency, President Carter said: "I promised you a president who is not isolated from the people, who feels your pain, and who shares your dreams, and who draws his strength and his wisdom from you." It obviously didn't do much for him, but since his time politicians have come to think that feeling people's pain—and even their own—in public is part of how the political game is played. "Politicians and public figures are under great pressure to discuss and reveal aspects of their hitherto private emotional life," Frank Furedi has written. "It is claimed that without making such a gesture, a public figure will fail to come across as human or approachable."[6]

This pressure is exerted primarily by the media for whom the first test of leadership has become the leader's capacity for feeling with or "empathizing" with the people. The worst thing that can be said about any politician in a democracy is that he is "isolated from the people" or, as it is more usually phrased, "out of touch" with those whose votes have put him in office. Assurances of feeling like Mr. Carter's, if not demonstrations of it, on a regular basis are needed to allay any fears of a public man's being out of touch. For a woman it's more complicated, as expressing her own private feelings can reinforce stereotypes about feminine weakness. But for men and women alike it has now become commonplace to rely on the vicarious, Carterite, "feel-your-pain" formula, particularly when it allows them to raise the curtain on some corner of their private life that the media can represent as a humanizing detail. Bill Clinton was adept at using the alleged hardships of his childhood and early youth for this purpose. His vice president, Al Gore, being from a more privileged background, used a serious accident to his son and the death of his sister—and his own feelings of love, compassion, and grief about these things—as a way of making a bid for political support, and the media's commitment to publicizing feeling would not allow them even to raise the question as to whether or not this use of the sufferings of others for political purposes was exploitative or cynical.[7]

Here is another parallel between the cult of feelings and that of objectivity, namely the taboo on looking into the partisan motivations of their adepts. When in mid-2007 the daringly outspoken Ann Coulter raised just this question about presidential candidate John Edwards's use on the campaign trail of personal tragedies—the death of his son and his wife's inoperable cancer—she was accused of "hate speech" by Mrs. Edwards, whose putative sufferings under Miss Coulter's lash then became further matter for sympathy for her from the media and from Mr. Edwards's political supporters. According to *The New York Times*, his donors substantially increased their level of support after Mrs. Edwards confronted Miss Coulter by telephone on a television show. Moreover, in doing so she also increased her own political credibility. "Mrs. Edwards," said the *Times*, "has . . . become a free operator on behalf of her husband of 29 years, a development that her friends suggest reflects the clarity and perspective that come from her cancer diagnosis, and her increasingly confident political instincts as she advises Mr. Edwards, a North Carolina Democrat, in his second White House bid."

The authors specifically cited as examples of her clarity of perspective and confident political instincts her willingness to confront Miss Coulter: "When Mrs. Edwards called in to a television talk show this week to confront the conservative commentator Ann Coulter who had attacked Mr. Edwards this year, it was a decision that Mrs. Edwards said she made impulsively and on her own."[8] Note that the authors of this very sympathetic piece make no mention of what Mr. Edwards had been attacked *about*. So committed are the media-mad to the drama and the romance of feelings as the real story behind political conflicts of all sorts— and the *Times* piece itself mentions Mrs. Edwards's cancer four more times in the course of its approximately 1,400 words—that even the possibility of an ulterior motive on the part either of their subjects or of themselves in the exposure of such feelings to the public gaze cannot be mentioned without putting oneself outside the ordinary bounds of political discourse.

THE COMMERCIAL USES OF CELEBRITY POLITICS

If celebrity journalism has not yet completely taken over the media's coverage of politics, it has gone far towards changing the political landscape. "He looked uncharacteristically dejected as he approached the lectern, fiddling with papers as he talked and avoiding the sort of winking eye contact he often makes with reporters," writes Peter Baker in *The Washington Post* of President George W. Bush after the failure of the immigration bill he had tried to push through Congress in the summer of 2007. "And then President Bush did something he almost never does: He admitted defeat."[9] The allusion in this opening paragraph of a front page "analysis" story was—as it was in so much of the *Post*'s reporting on the Bush administration after 2003—to what the author regards as the president's failure in Iraq. That the immigration bill had in fact and demonstrably failed while the war in Iraq was still going on and, to the president if not to Mr. Baker, was still a matter for debate mattered not at all. To the media-mad, Iraq was already a "defeat"—and one which the president was stubbornly refusing to "admit." See how useful the media are to us? Without them to infer the feelings behind the president's words and put them into the context of the media's own master narrative of the Bush presidency— a story of intellectual and moral as well as political and military failure unsuccessfully masked by a stiff-necked (and "out of touch") failure to acknowledge it—we might not know that the war was as lost as the immigration bill.

Biased? Sure. But the point ought to be that the bias is not, or not just, a matter of political parties, however sure we are—and, as we saw in the last chapter, we can be pretty sure—that the media are overwhelmingly Democratic in their sympathies. Media madness goes beyond bias. It arises out of everything the media are and do and how they see themselves and their role. When we buy in to the psychodrama of feelings and hidden realities beneath political or other appearances, we are biased too, and our access to reality is limited by our acceptance of the media's model of it. The media could hardly exist as a paying proposition without the assumption, which they have been very successful in fostering among the population at large, that political reality and appearance must always be at variance, and that our access through the thickets of appearance to the realities behind them must depend on our willingness to trust them to know, through laborious digging, the way through.

I shall have more to say about reality and "reality" in Chapter Three, but here I want to notice something else about that commercial model, which is the competitive advantage it gives to those who are in a position to take advantage of big media's economies of scale. The media have made the values of the celebrity culture their own because celebrity sells, but celebrity sells partly because it is able to limit access to itself. This obviously gives the commercial media a huge advantage over the blogger and other unofficial media. They can either pay for access or, what is much more common, they can use their large audiences as leverage to get access to celebrities who have something to sell—a book, a movie, a television show, or a cause. That's why causes and celebrities are so keen on each other: the cause can use its celebrity spokespeople to gain a mass audience for itself while the celebrities enhance their celebrity status by showing that they "care"—about AIDS orphans or the rain forest or land mines or global warming or whatever it is that the media themselves have certified to be a good cause.

FEELINGS, VICTIMHOOD, AND THE CELBRITY "EXPERT"

We know that these are good causes partly, at least, on the grounds that they are causing anguish to celebrities, in whose feelings we have long been accustomed to take a keen interest. And because celebrities are just like us in their feelings, similar feelings or even more intense ones can make celebrities of those who have such feelings, at least if they are of the right kind. Cindy Sheehan, for instance, has no more insight or understanding about the reasons why America went to war in Iraq than any random woman pulled off the street, but she has become an expert on Iraq, and someone whom President Bush can be criticized for not listening to, by suffering the loss of a son there. Michael Moore adopted the same technique in his circus-like "documentary" *Fahrenheit 9/11* allowing the mother of a son killed in the war to be his chief spokesman against it.

Hardly anyone—at least hardly anyone in the media— saw in this any trace of exploitation or disingenuousness on the part of the anti-warriors any more than they do in Mrs.

Edwards's frequent mentions of her cancer diagnosis. To do so would be to be guilty of "mean-spiritedness," if not the "hate speech" that Ann Coulter was accused of. When she was asked by Jeremy Paxman of the BBC's "Newsnight" if she would withdraw derogatory comments she had made about 9/11 widows, Ann Coulter replied: "No, I think you can save all the would-you-like-to-withdraw questions, but you could quote me accurately. I didn't write about the 9/11 widows. I wrote about four widows cutting campaign commercials for John Kerry and using the fact that their husbands died on 9/11 to prevent anyone from responding."

In the liberal *New Republic*'s online version, Elspeth Reeve was somewhat abashed at this and couldn't help admitting: "The thing is . . . it's kind of true. A little. It is a little absurd to hold up a person as an expert judge of the 9/11 Commission Report, for example, just because she lost a loved one. Liberals do tend to do that kind of thing, and it makes us look like weenies."[10] There was a rare moment of self-knowledge, but for the most part, the unquenchable appetite for emotion makes for as few compunctions on the part of the media-mad as on that of the afflicted who seek to take advantage of that appetite to advance a cause or a candidate. Such influence with the media can be taken for granted as one of the perks of suffering, particularly where the suffering, like that of the bereaved of 9/11, has been in any degree public already. The media regard the views of such people on war and terrorism as being intrinsically valuable, though of course they have no special knowledge of the geopolitical circumstances that have produced these things either.

In the same way, a father whose son was stillborn because of the distance to the nearest hospital is asked for his views on hospital closures; the mother or the wife of a murder victim is asked about crime or the mother of a child killed by a speeding driver about traffic regulations. As Carol Sarler wrote in *The Times* of London, "the truth is that not one of these people has any better insight into such momentous issues" as what should be done about hospital closures or how to deal with violent criminals or speeders than anyone else.

> Prurient media, together with their prurient clientele, have elevated victims to the status of experts, making pundits of people based on absolutely nothing beyond their suffering, which at best achieves no more than the chance of a temporary catharsis for them, and at worst pushes aside the voices of the duller, but better-informed—hospital managers, criminologists, psychologists among them—whose proper expertise could more sensibly inform policy and change. There is a great clamour for victims' voices to be heard and, if it helps them, we should listen. But we cannot accept an expression of pain to be a substitute for knowledge. Quite the reverse: it is the hardest thing in the world to be rational, fair or sane when you hurt.[11]

This might seem to be obvious, but media madness is far more interested in hurt than it is in rationality, fairness or sanity. A front-page *Washington Post* story on an anti-war blogger, Maryscott O'Connor, quotes her as saying: "I'm insane with rage and grief," apparently regarding this as a reason to take her and her views seriously instead of a reason not to take them seriously.[12]

What makes the likes of Cindy Sheehan or Maryscott O'Connor into celebrity experts—that is, those whose feelings on a particular subject are of intrinsic interest and not because of anything original or especially insightful that they might have to say about it—is the authenticity that their suffering is popularly supposed to confer upon them. But that authenticity, we notice, only works one way. A bereaved parent or a passionate blogger who supported the war would not be of any great interest to the media—not only because the media themselves tend to share the opinions of those who are anti-war but also because the opinions of anyone who in the same circumstances was pro-war would have to represent at least to some extent a *denial* of feeling, a refusal to allow natural feelings of grief or anger or resentment over the human costs of the war to determine their view of it. The belief that feelings should be disciplined rather than yielded to is the sin against the media spirit that cannot be forgiven. However sympathetic we may be to this emphasis on authenticity of feeling, we must admit that it gives us a partial and a distorted view of any subject that is also susceptible to rational analysis.

For commercial reasons too, the media have sought to become a manufactory of celebrity, which is the reason for shows like "American Idol" and the numerous "reality" series that came to dominate the television networks in the late 1990s. The same procedures can be seen at work in their coverage of politics. The demand for celebrity is matched against a potentially infinite supply, and anyone can become an expert—and a celebrity—if he's saying what the media want to hear. Obviously this becomes an all-but irresistible temptation to disgruntled former officials who find themselves, whether by accident or design, aligned with the media's view of official behavior. Just ask Richard Clarke, the former adviser on terrorism to both Bill Clinton and George W. Bush who parlayed his disagreements with the latter into a bestselling book, a movie deal, and the depiction of himself in more than one work of fiction as a folk hero.

The ease with which the media are able to find such supposed experts who are ready and willing to expose what they can sell as the reality behind official appearances is also partly a consequence of their penchant for second-guessing. The media's default assumption is that, whenever anything bad happens, whether a hurricane or a terrorist attack, someone must be at fault for not having prevented or at least foreseen it. Moreover, there's not much that happens that somebody has not foreseen, even if only by chance. All the media have to do is find out such a person and hail him or her as an unjustly neglected prophet—an expert and a suffering celebrity all rolled into one. Sometimes, as in Mr. Clarke's case, it is enough for the prophet to have foreseen the disaster only in the most general terms. At the time when he was being fanatical about the terrorist threat, almost nobody else was. By the time he came to public attention, almost nobody was again, except for the Bush administration whom he criticized for not being fanatical enough! But the media, who were the reverse of fanatical themselves, were prepared to criticize the administration simultaneously for being as apathetic as themselves before 9/11 and for being much less apathetic afterwards.

———

INTELLIGENCE A FUNCTION OF CONTEXT

The war in Iraq has made it a latter-day journalistic cliché to charge the Bush administration with "cherry-picking" the intelligence data in order to justify its case for going to war in 2003,[13] and yet this is just a pejorative way of describing what government and media alike do all the time and what *they can't help doing*. Intelligence tells us too many conflicting things for the process of picking out the parts of it which we guess are true to be perspicuous. The narrative that we construct for ourselves out of the conflicting data will therefore be the product of bias, which everyone has but the denial of which in their own case is the foundation on which the mass media's house has been built. That denial has as one of its corollaries the absurd refusal to examine the motivations of those who, without such an examination, are in a position to exploit and manipulate the media. Leakers of confidential information, for instance, or political opponents of the administration within the bureaucracy or those who, like Ambassador Joseph Wilson, could plausibly claim to be its disillusioned supporters, are just as sure to have their own reasons for wanting their privileged information made public as the administration is sure to have theirs for suppressing it, but the media routinely privilege the leak (or the statement of opposition) over the official version of the truth just because it is unofficial.

This means that the media version of events must be cut to fit the Procrustean bed of the media's expectations, so that really quite interesting stories which don't fit it are completely ignored. In the Plame-Wilson, story, for instance, and in the media's coverage of the trial of I. Lewis "Scooter"

Libby which followed, the need to cast the story as a Bush administration scandal, an instance of putative misbehavior not only on Mr. Libby's part but on that of the vice president and the president themselves, made the media miss completely a potentially much bigger story and perhaps an even more scandalous one. This was that the Central Intelligence Agency has gone out of the administration's control. Why should White House staff be briefing against the Agency unless the Agency were already briefing—as journalists very well knew it was at least as early as the 2004 election campaign—against the White House? The appointment of Porter Goss as Director of Central Intelligence in that year—together with the establishment of the new post of Director of National Intelligence and the appointment to it of John Negroponte in 2005—was pretty obviously an attempt by the administration to bring the Agency back into line. Mr. Goss's abrupt departure less than two years later was, equally obviously, a sign of that attempt's failure.

Ambassador Wilson's criticisms in *The New York Times* in the summer of 2003 should have been seen as an early evidence of a dangerous bureaucratic rift within the government, but because the media took them at face value and were barred by their own mythologies from questioning the ambassador's motives as well as the administration's, they missed it. The affair was also further evidence, if any further evidence were needed, that the bias of press and public alike is now as surely in favor of believing the scandal mongers as it once was in favor of believing the elected leaders of the country—a breakdown in trust that the media are able to exploit for their own gain, though seldom to notice as a cause for public concern in its own right. Having abandoned traditional ideas of discretion, decorum, national security, and any other limitations on their capacity to make things public—that would now be described as "self-censorship" (or "censorship" *tout court*)—they are no longer in any position to exercise real judgment in the matter of putting information in context. The context is instead the crude and ready-made one of wrongdoing by the powerful that the media justify their own existence by seeking to uncover.

Other contexts must always be suspect to those who stake a claim to objectivity, since context is interpretation and not fact. News "analysis" provides a limited space within which to sketch in context, but most context defaults to simple scandalology. The media-mad fail to understand this because they see themselves as being in the business of making *everything* public. In fact, they are in the business of making *anything* public, which is a very different thing. If it were everything, rather than anything, that they were prepared to show us, then we might be able to get a whole picture, which also would be a complete context for any given use of data. That's the only way we could truly tell when someone was "cherry-picking" or "exploiting" data in an illegitimate way. If we could see everything, then there would be no difficulty about making up our minds what to think about it.

But, of course, that's just it. We can't. There will always be things missing from any picture, no matter how carefully limned: things that remain invisible either because someone has successfully prevented them from exposure to the public eye or because they didn't seem important to the person painting the picture. That's why it is always the painter's version of reality that we see and not reality itself. But one corollary of their claims both to objectivity and to the guardianship of authentic feeling is that the media-mad can also claim to be in touch with "reality" in a way in which others are not. They have no trouble assuming—by the charge of "cherry-picking" for example—that they can see reality whole and, therefore, that anyone who doesn't see it the way they see it must be "delusional." Some of the consequences of this arrogant point of view will be the subject of our next chapter.

3 | The Language of Hyperbole and the Manufacture of Reality

"Going too far is half th' pleasure of not getting anywhere."
—Zippy the Pinhead[1]

WHEN BILL DEDMAN of MSNBC revealed in an article about the political contributions of journalists[2] that Mark Singer of *The New Yorker* had donated $250 to John Kerry's "Victory Campaign, 2004," Mr. Singer explained his presumptive breach of journalistic etiquette as follows:

> Probably there should be a rule against it. But there's a rule against murder. If someone had murdered Hitler —a journalist interviewing him had murdered him— the world would be a better place. I only feel good, as a citizen, about getting rid of George Bush, who has been the most destructive President in my lifetime. I certainly don't regret it.[3]

Hitler? No, no. Hitler wasn't so bad as George Bush, at least not according to Peter Mehlman, formerly of *The Washington Post* and "Seinfeld" and now blogging for the Huffington Post.

> You could argue that even the world's worst fascist dictators at least meant well. They honestly thought

45

were doing good things for their countries by suppressing blacks/eliminating Jews/eradicating free
enterprise/repressing individual thought/ killing off
rivals/invading neighbors, etc.... Bush set a new
precedent. He came into office with the attitude of
"I'm so tired of the public good. What about my
good? What about my rich friends' good?"[4]

According to Keith Ellison, Democratic member of Congress from Minnesota, President Bush even had his own
Reichstag fire in the burning towers of 9/11. At least that's
what terror attacks by fanatical Muslims reminded America's first Muslim congressman of.[5] Nor was the tenor of his
partisanship necessarily religiously motivated. I recently
received a brochure in which former Vice President Al Gore
wrote on behalf of the Democratic Senatorial Campaign
Committee and urged me to send money on the grounds
that "George Bush has destroyed America as we know it,
and only by keeping a Democratic Senate can we undo the
damage."

Is it possible that even the most fervently believing
Democrats actually believe such stuff? Or is wild hyperbole,
as Zippy the Pinhead suggests, just one of the consolations
of being out of office—as it was among some Republicans
during the Clinton years? In any case, it has become not just
a useful tool for fundraising but, on account of media madness, to a worrying extent the common currency of politics
in our time. Did the politicians learn it from the media or
the media learn it from the politicians? It may be a chicken-
and-egg problem, but I'm inclined to believe that the media
have the priority because it is so much more obviously in

their interests than it is in those of the politicians thus to pitch the dramas of ordinary political confrontation at such apocalyptic levels.

Either way, even the most thoughtful controversialists may fall victim to the temptations of rhetorical extremism. During the election campaign of 2006, Peter Beinart of *The New Republic* accused the Bush administration of "McCarthyism" for suggesting that Democratic men and measures in power would endanger national security.[6] Presumably the president really believes that this is true. Why would he propose different security measures if he thought those which the Democrats proposed were perfectly okay? He wasn't making anything up or slandering anyone with false accusations of subversive intent. Yet for putting his own political position before the public, and saying he thought it was worthy of electoral support because he believed it would contribute more to American security than the alternative, he gets whacked with the charge of "McCarthyism."

Likewise, for speaking openly about the importance of religious faith in his life, he is accused by the likes of the ex-Republican activist Kevin Phillips of seeking to establish a "theocracy."[7] Maureen Dowd of *The New York Times*, appearing on the NBC television show "Meet the Press," claimed that President Bush had "merged church and state" in America while trying to keep them apart in Iraq.[8]

Not even Maureen Dowd can seriously imagine that the man she so despises has "merged" church and state—even if we assume that what she really meant was not "church" but "religious belief." Such hyperbole is born of the confidence of the media-mad, and it is particularly at home in the pages of *The New York Times*, which enjoys a certain community of understanding with its audience. Neither Maureen Dowd nor Frank Rich nor Paul Krugman nor those who write the *Times*'s editorials give the impression that they have seriously considered the arguments of those who disagree with them. It's too easy for them to assume that their readers think as they do and so won't mind getting vulgar abuse in place of argument. After six years of the Bush administration, they give the appearance of belonging to a sort of club of which one of the conditions of membership is a willingness to believe anything at all to the discredit of the president. The theocracy is just one of the hyperbolical pleasantries that exist in what we might call *media-reality*—which it then becomes another point in the indictment of Mr. Bush that he is "out of touch" with or even "in denial" about.

Who Gets to Decide What "Reality" Is?

Shortly before the presidential election of 2004, Ron Suskind, the former reporter for *The Wall Street Journal* who ghostwrote the memoir by President Bush's disgruntled first treasury secretary, Paul O'Neill, wrote in *The New York Times Magazine* of a conversation he said he had had with an unnamed "senior adviser" of the Bush administration. The adviser told him something which "at the time I didn't fully comprehend—but I now believe gets to the very heart of the Bush presidency."

> The aide said that guys like me were "in what we call the reality-based community," which he defined as people who "believe that solutions emerge from your judicious study of discernible reality." I nodded and

murmured something about enlightenment principles and empiricism. He cut me off. "That's not the way the world really works anymore," he continued. "We're an empire now, and when we act, we create our own reality. And while you're studying that reality—judiciously, as you will—we'll act again, creating other new realities, which you can study too, and that's how things will sort out. We're history's actors . . . and you, all of you, will be left to just study what we do."⁹

So far as I know, this aide has never been identified, nor has anyone in the White House either acknowledged that these words or something like them were ever said or, if they were said, attempted to explain their meaning. It is apparently White House policy—or it was at least through the 2004 election—not to answer even the most scurrilous or easily refuted charges made against it by the president's political enemies. But the rest of those enemies must have been more quickly persuaded than Mr. Suskind had been that they could "fully comprehend" the meaning of a phrase like "the reality-based community," since it was used over and over again, especially by left-leaning bloggers—who would advertise themselves as "a proud member of the reality-based community"—and *New York Times* columnists and editorialists both before and after the election.¹⁰ The aide's remark seemed to flatter the self-conceit of the media-mad as purveyors of reality and to provide a justification for the view that the media's idea of "reality" was in fact reality while the president's was, well, something else. In other words, so many people seized on the phrase because they saw how it could be treated as a frank admission that he and the entire administration of which he was a part were delusional.

Leave aside the logical conundrum of how far we can trust the accuracy and clear-sightedness of someone, on the subject of his own delusions or on any other, who admits to being delusional. Whatever else the aide said or meant, it is scarcely possible that he could have meant what Mr. Suskind and many others in the media affected to believe he meant; nor do I see how we can be expected to be much impressed with the sense of reality of anyone who supposes he could have meant it. Even within the quotation, we can see that the aide's saying "That's not the way the world *really* works" or "we create our own reality," must mean that the word "reality" in the phrase "the reality-based community" ought to have had quotation marks around it. He must, that is, have been using the term ironically. But by not dealing with his words on their own terms—by, in effect, removing the quotation marks and pretending to suppose that the aide and who knew how many others in the administration meant what he means by "reality," namely what the president is out of touch with—Mr. Suskind was essentially demonstrating the truth of what seems to me likely to have been the aide's actual point: that *media-reality* is not reality at all.

By the time of the 2006 midterm elections this theme— that President Bush individually or his administration collectively were out of touch with reality, "in denial," and sometimes even "delusional" about the problems they were attempting to deal with, especially the war in Iraq—became ubiquitous among the media-mad. Leading the pack were the third installment of Bob Woodward's "Bush at War"

series, which he titled *State of Denial*,[11] and the editorial
and op-ed pages of *The New York Times*. In response to the
president's claim that "the United States and its friends are
holding firm in a battle that will decide whether freedom or
terror will rule the twenty-first century," for example, the
Times editorialized, "If that were actual reality, the president's call to 'put aside our differences and work together to
meet the test that history has given us' would be inspiring,
instead of frustrating and depressing."[12]

And why is it frustrating and depressing? Why is it not
"actual reality"? Because, the *Times* insists, "Iraq had nothing
to do with the war on terror until the Bush administration
decided to invade it."[13] I find it almost touching, this kind of
faith in the one paramount fact about the Iraq war that so
many in the media see as explaining everything about it. For
the media-mad, time is frozen in May of 2003 when President Bush landed on the flight deck of the aircraft carrier
USS Abraham Lincoln and gave his now famous speech—
not famous as a speech but famous as a media event—under
a banner reading "Mission Accomplished."[14] It was at that
point when, retrospectively, the invasion of Iraq could be
regarded as a definitive mistake, and therefore when it was
most in conformity with the view of it which the media have
since decided is "reality."

For the sake of argument, let us stipulate that it was a
mistake. Let us even ignore, for the moment, the fact that
if there had been no Iraqi involvement in the events of
9/11, Saddam Hussein's Iraq had been very far from having
"nothing to do with the war on terror" before the invasion.[15]
The mistakenness of the invasion itself was a fact of ever-
decreasing relevance to the war that was being fought in

"actual reality" in September of 2006 when *State of Denial* was released and is still being fought as I write. Iraq certainly has everything to do with the war on terror today, since that is where the terrorists and the Bush administration have agreed to fight it most intensely. The latter may have chosen the battlefield unwisely—I, for one, happen to think so—but the reality that it *is* the battlefield, now and for the foreseeable future, would seem undeniable to anyone not trapped in the bubble of media reality that has been created out of intellectual pride, wisdom after the fact, and unbridled hyperbole.

THE MAD EMPEROR AND HIS DASTARDLY HENCHMAN

With his usual taste for the theatrical, Frank Rich in December 2006 suggested that

> we've been reading the wrong Bob Woodward book to understand what's going on with President Bush. The text we should be consulting instead is *The Final Days*, the Woodward-Bernstein account of Richard Nixon talking to the portraits on the White House walls while Watergate demolished his presidency. As Mr. Bush has ricocheted from Vietnam to Latvia to Jordan in recent weeks, we've witnessed the troubling behavior of a president who isn't merely in a state of denial but is completely untethered from reality. It's not that he can't handle the truth about Iraq. He doesn't know what the truth is.[16]

On closer examination, we found that Mr. Rich was basing his claim that the president was a victim of mental illness on the assumption that his public speech—for instance his expressions of confidence in the government of Prime Minister Nuri al-Maliki of Iraq—was an infallible indicator of his private feelings. It was a particularly odd assumption on the part of someone who, on other occasions, has not scrupled to accuse Mr. Bush of mendacity—who, indeed, had just published a book grandly if preposterously titled *The Greatest Story Ever Sold: The Decline and Fall of Truth From 9/11 to Katrina*[17] which had treated "truth" with the same hyperbolical casualness that he treats "reality" here. In both cases, he scarcely bothers to disguise the fact that these words mean nothing more to him than "what I think," which can only be owing to the poetic license that the media culture so readily affords him and others who abide by its conventions.

As it was hardly possible that Mr. Rich did not know of the military and diplomatic constraints under which the president's public utterances, like those of any political leader, had been formulated, it was hard not to suppose a certain disingenuousness on his part, to say the least, in rushing to his diagnosis of psychotic behavior on such flimsy grounds, but the media consensus of an administration "out of touch" or "in denial" was over two years old at that point—it had become almost a cliché—so that the standard of evidence required for further demonstration of a fact so obvious was not very high. Once established, it then gave rise to a further genre of stories explaining the psychological mechanisms of "denial" in general and—sometimes more in sorrow than in Richian anger—how it had happened that

President Bush or those around him had fallen victim to it.[18] Hyperbole was by this time generating its own hyperbole, as when Maureen Dowd wrote that "delusional is far too mild a word to describe Dick Cheney. Delusional doesn't begin to capture the profound, transcendental one-flew-over daftness of the man."[19] In other words, her previous absurd overstatement is now inoperative and should be regarded as an absurd understatement. On another occasion she wrote that "It's hard to imagine how Dick Cheney could get more dastardly,"[20] a statement so obviously untrue—has he started violating virgins or boiling babies yet?—as to suggest, like the word "dastardly," a certain self-consciousness, even self-satire, about her slipping on the mask of outrage. But that sort of *jeu d'esprit* comes out like the wit it is obviously intended to be in the fantasy world of media reality.

"Lies," Insults, and Tautologies

If we look back again to the origins of this conceit in Mr. Suskind's *New York Times Magazine* article, the credulity of the media-mad in believing anything so ridiculously im-plausible as that they had on record a confession by the Bush administration to being out of touch with reality is reminiscent of Dan Rather's gullibility in seizing upon forged documents to raise a scandal about President Bush's military record.[21] In both cases, the eagerness to believe in something surely arises out of its fitting so well with the media's own assumptions about the world. It also fits in with the media's conceit of itself as "objective," which I dis-cussed in Chapter One. If someone imagines himself as entitled to define "reality" as part of a larger rhetorical strategy, it helps if he has first learned to think of himself as "objective." The opposite of "objective" for the media-mad is "partisan." They believe that, to be a "partisan"—like most Republicans but not like those who believe as they do—is to be in some degree reality-blind. If a Republican seems to confirm this, the media-mad will only take it as their due.

The word "reality" as used by the media carries the same import as it does in "reality T V"—which is to say that, whatever else it means, it cannot mean reality. And for the same reason: namely that the camera lens distorts. Caught in the media spotlight, reality mugs and preens and strikes attitudes just like everybody else. With reality television, the word implies something mildly shocking but not surprising. Though the reality show is unscripted, we expect it to produce something familiar—especially a state of heightened emotion and manifestations of shame and intrigue when this leads to anger, greed, lust, or jealousy. It is by these emotions that we are able to recognize it as reality. It's the same with the "reality" that the media sees where they imagine those they report on—especially politicians—do not see it. The "reality" (in this sense) of the war in Iraq, for instance, is only recognizable as such insofar as it testifies to (among other things) the ineradicability of the insurgency, the devotion and determination of its adherents, and the hopelessness of the Bush administration's efforts to pacify it.

These things, of course, may be true. Or they may not be. But true or not, they necessarily constitute the media's "reality." You might almost say that reality, as the media-mad are accustomed to using the term, can be defined as what the administration does not (officially, at any rate) believe. Therefore, when the media say that the administration—

and this would be true to a greater or lesser extent of any administration—is out of touch with reality it is a tautology. That is to say that, by the terms under which the media culture has become established, it is the administration's job to be out of touch with reality just as it is the media's job to point the fact out to us. If the politicians were capable of apprehending reality for themselves, there would be no high-minded task for the media to perform, no speaking truth to power, of the sort which, since Watergate and Vietnam, they have seen it as their job to perform. And it is structurally necessary for the media to tell a different story from the administration's story as much as it is for them to claim "objectivity" or a privileged access to private feelings. It follows that the administration must either be stupid or corrupt—or, of course, both—for believing anything different.

The media-mad, who now also dominate the political opposition, tend to be divided on the question of which it is, stupidity or corruption. Many on the left write or speak as if the mantra of the more vocal sections of the anti-war movement, "Bush lied/People died," could be taken for granted, though evidence of actual bad faith—as opposed to mistakes in judgment—has never been forthcoming. The most frequently cited example of presidential mendacity, the danger from weapons of mass destruction in Iraq, is a particularly feeble one as, if the administration knew that there were no such weapons, it hardly made sense to lie about it in order to justify an action whose success was itself guaranteed to expose the lie. And even if we suppose a fiendish, sort of double-dyed Machiavellianism—what price stupidity now? —which counted on people's making just that argument, that they could not have been so stupid, there has never been an iota of evidence that anyone in the administration knew what, otherwise, no one in the world outside of Iraq knew in March of 2003.

But the media's rhetorical conventions are quite undemanding when it comes to charges of lying against our nation's leaders, which is what leads to the media madness of a Paul Krugman, when he described, in his op-ed page column in the *Times*, then-presidential candidate George W. Bush's performance in one of his debates with Al Gore in 2000

> Throughout that debate, George W. Bush made blatantly misleading statements, including some outright lies—for example, when he declared of his tax cut that "the vast majority of the help goes to the people at the bottom end of the economic ladder." That should have told us, right then and there, that he was not a man to be trusted.[22]

To call this a lie is at least as much a political and partisan act as Mr. Bush's statement was in the first place. "Help" here, the latter could have argued, should be taken as a relative term. A small amount of money is likely to be more "help" to a person "at the bottom end of the economic ladder" than quite a large amount of money is to someone at the other end. Moreover, if the latter invests the money, its marginal benefit ("help") to him is arguably less than that of the job opportunities his investment creates are to the former. It may have been a mistake on candidate Bush's part to believe this—Prof. Krugman, an economist, would presumably say it was—but that does not mean that it is a lie. The professor is understandably proud of his academic accomplishments and the knowledge that they betoken, but it is media madness and not academic authority which allows him tacitly to suppose that there is no possible opinion apart from his own as to where the principal benefits of an economic or tax policy are likely to flow, and that anyone who holds another opinion on the subject must acting in bad faith.

Mr. Rich, Miss Dowd, and the other denizens of *The New York Times* op-ed and editorial pages are perhaps among the more extreme cases of those who think their own opinions correspond to "reality," though none of them is more cocksure about it than Prof. Krugman who sees himself as reality's trustee even when the ranks of the deluded and mendacious are expanded to include not just the Republicans in power but also those who aspire to power:

> Here's the way it ought to be [he wrote in a May, 2007 column]: When Rudy Giuliani says that Iran, which had nothing to do with 9/11, is part of a "movement" that "has already displayed more aggressive tendencies by coming here and killing us," he should be treated as a lunatic.
>
> When Mitt Romney says that a coalition of "Shia and Sunni and Hezbollah and Hamas and the Muslim Brotherhood and Al Qaeda" wants to "bring down the West," he should be ridiculed for his ignorance.
>
> And when John McCain says that Osama, who isn't in Iraq, will "follow us home" if we leave, he should be laughed at.[23]

He must surely know that it is not just lunatics and fools who believe these things but a great many serious students of the war on terror—to say nothing of millions of ordinary Americans.

Yet the fact that there is no natural check on the media's ability to define reality according to its own beliefs and assumptions means that it becomes easy for them to assume that it must be the politicians who are out of touch with reality, not themselves. "On the dominant issue of our time, the president is in denial," wrote Dan Froomkin in *The Washington Post*. "By most reliable accounts, three and a half years into the U.S. occupation, Iraq is in chaos—if not in a state of civil war, then awfully close. But President Bush insists it's not so." [24]

The president had been answering a question from Wolf Blitzer of CNN who had quoted to him Kofi Annan's belief that Iraq was, at that time (September 2006), on the brink of "full-scale civil war." Mr. Bush, citing the opinions of his generals and civilian officials on the ground in Iraq had denied that this was the case. Now I find it just a little bit difficult to believe that Dan Froomkin *really* thinks this denial amounts to being "in denial" or that the only way the president could have demonstrated that he was not deranged was to have answered his questioner, "Yes, Wolf, I have to admit that Iraq has fallen into chaos and civil war and that my administration has made a complete hash of the operation on which I have staked my entire presidency. I'll be resigning tomorrow." If the *Post*'s commentator does believe this, then he is the one living in a fantasy world. But whether he believes it or not, he has made a journalistic nothing into something by relying on the tacit assumption that it is the media—because politicians are always covering up things—who get to decide what reality is.

It is itself a sign of detachment from reality to suppose that the President of the United States—*any* president of the United States—is clueless about the things that are so plain to his journalistic critics. The media-mad themselves admit the improbability of such a state of affairs when they are reduced to using the language of pop-psychologizing, as Mr. Froomkin does here, to suggest that such cluelessness can only be owing to a state ("in denial") that borders on the psychotic. The importance of psychotherapeutic assumptions to the media worldview is a subject to which I shall return in Chapter Five, but here it is worth noticing that such attempts as this one to medicalize policy differences are analogous to the criminalization of such differences (which the media also encourage by promoting scandal wherever they can find it) in the assumption that only one way of looking at a subject—political, diplomatic, or military—is possible.

The same assumption is evident when Mr. Froomkin goes on, observing that the president "says the people he talks to assure him that the press coverage about how bad things are in Iraq is not to be trusted." Here is the only hard bit of information in the piece, though even that is something that we could have guessed for ourselves. In other words, the president's sources in Iraq—i.e., U.S. armed forces and government personnel—have a different picture of the Iraqi reality than Mr. Froomkin's—i.e., the media's. Now you'd think that the next step for any conscientious reporter would be to ask the obvious question: Which of these two pictures of reality, the government's or the media's, is likely to be closer to the truth? There are things to be said in favor of both. On the one hand, the government view is likely to be skewed by the bureaucratic impulse of those on the ground in Iraq as well as those back in Washington to minimize their own responsibility for failure; on the other hand, the view of the media is likely to be skewed by the need to get a good story in order to sell their news product (and disaster always makes for better stories than success) and by their near-universal hostility towards President Bush. But Dan Froomkin not only does not ask that question, he doesn't even think of asking it. The conventions of the media culture have by now hardened into mere assumptions, and among these is the assumption that anything the media decides is reality is reality.

Living in Media Reality

There is perhaps more than a hint in the "reality"-mongering of the media-mad of the philosophy of the late Jean Baudrillard, whose theorizing that media-reality is the only reality we can truly know once led him to claim, in his playful, postmodern fashion, that "The Gulf War Did Not Happen." Likewise, he later averred that the destruction of the World Trade Center on September 11, 2001, was essentially a "dark fantasy" created by the media, since in reality (or whatever he supposed was the opposite of fantasy in a media-created world of "hyperreality" dominated by "simulacra") the victims were already as good as dead before the airplanes hit the towers, so horrible were they, undestroyed, in their architectural, political, and economic consequences.[25] Though not intended as flattery, such an elevation of the importance of the media could obviously be taken as such. The offer, however ironical, of a proprietorial interest in reality also has tremendous commercial implications, but it could only be taken up by the media to the extent that they continue to disguise from themselves that they inhabit a rhetorical world of their own, a world ironically remote from that of ordinary people in what is still occasionally referred to as "the real world."

That's why the hyperbole is not just a matter of Bush-bashing. For the media-mad, it is a way of life. Here, for instance, is what the columnist Eugene Robinson of *The Washington Post*, thought of the immigration bill of 2007:

> It's also accurate to point out, however, that those 12 million or so people are already settled here, that for the most part they are doing jobs our society wants done, and that any serious attempt to drive them out of the country—even "temporarily," so they could apply to be let back in—would be indistinguishable from a pogrom.[26]

There is always the possibility, of course, that neither Mr. Robinson nor his editors knows the meaning of the words "indistinguishable" and "pogrom," which could explain their ludicrous misuse here. But that is simply another way of saying that they feel entitled to be careless with language —as do so many other employers of rhetorically unconstrained hyperbole. The club to which they belong, the club of the media mad, is devoted to bashing President Bush *ex officio*, but it is not very likely that it will find a shortage of others to bash when he leaves office.

Membership in the club of Bush haters is made additionally attractive by offering as one of its fringe benefits a social certification of one's intelligence. At least as much as in their hatred of the president, the club is united in the assumption that its members see things more clearly than he does and therefore that *anyone* who disagrees with them is likely to be either stupid or mendacious and corrupt. In an extreme case, like that of Richard Cohen of *The Washington Post*, the hubris of such a point of view will even lead a man to pronounce that "this country has a bunch of fools for leaders." [27] That is both Republicans *and* Democrats have demonstrated their profound lack of intelligence by failing to be guided by the trenchant analyses of the problems of the day delivered from far above the merely "partisan" battle by R. Cohen. The complete absence of any sense of irony in making such a media-mad statement as that is one indication of the extent to which it is really the media who are "out of touch." And yet, they are so not because they are "delusional" but because political opinions are for them also tribal identifications and, as such, a way of making a claim to social status and honor.

4 | Intelligence and Status: The Great Scandal Hunt

NOT LONG AGO, the Marxist scholar and *homme de lettres* Terry Eagleton led off an article proclaiming his aversion to electronic mail with the following rhetorical flourish: "Just as George Bush shows that you don't need a brain to rule the world, so I am living proof that nobody needs e-mail."[1] *Just* as? Is this meant to be a joke? It looks like one to anyone not accustomed to the profoundly conventional nature of journalistic language. Inside the media's rhetorical cocoon, however, the proposition that President Bush is stupid, even imbecilic, is a commonplace on the order of saying that the sky is blue or the grass is green. It's not a joke. Or perhaps it's beyond a joke. For this commonplace has become a literary topos for improvising on, a musical theme for playing variations on—as when Mr. Bush's fellow Texan, the talk-show host Jim Hightower, found his way into future anthologies of media wit by saying that "if ignorance ever goes to $40 a barrel, I want drilling rights on George Bush's head." This was actually said about the second President Bush's father, but I have seen it quoted[2] as if it had been said about the son —an easy transference because the witty aspersion cast upon the intelligence of Republican politicians has long been a commonplace among patrician Democrats and those who wish to be thought like them. So many repetitions, with variations, of the same idea hardly seem necessary, but they are also useful for putting the audience on notice as to the writer's or speaker's membership in a particular universe of discourse. Next to that essential fact about it, the truth or falsity of the idea itself seems almost irrelevant.

The trope of the president's stupidity is another instance of the use of hyperbole by the media-mad discussed in the last chapter, as well as a manifestation of the phenomena I noticed in the first and second chapters—the driving out of fairness by the pretense of objectivity and the assumption of the media's access to hidden and invariably discreditable truths about the powerful which they would have wished to keep hidden. Doubtless those who play with it as Prof. Eagleton does really do believe that the presidential IQ is (at best) sub-normal, but whether they do or not they have a rhetorical interest in claiming to believe it because it is a corollary of their belief in the obviousness of the choices involved in governing. The subtext is that you would have to be a complete idiot to have made the choices that President Bush has made. The right choices—not his, obviously—were there for anyone to see, and yet he somehow managed to overlook them. Those in the media may know in their hearts that this is not fair to the terrible realities of political decisionmaking, but perhaps they feel they can rely on the pretense of objectivity to override that sense of fairness.

All of this information is packed into Prof. Eagleton's witticism, and yet it retains the overtones of humorous hyperbole that those outside that universe hear, and this creates a certain rhetorical dislocation. Certainly the professor cannot really suppose that the president doesn't have a brain or that he rules the world, but, if he doesn't suppose these things, is his hyperbole also meant to extend ("just as") to the proposition that nobody needs e-mail? The more you think about the analogy, the odder it seems. Presumably, you're not supposed to think about it. The routine use of hyperbole which is uncontained by a meaningful context—as when a writer or speaker makes it clear that his exaggeration is only for comic effect—creates a fantasy world which, by a sort of self-denying irony, an author invites his readers to live in as a way of proclaiming a partisan alliance—one that others are encouraged to join by sharing this joke which they pretend is not a joke. Thus Joseph Biden, one of those candidates for the presidency whose chief disqualification for the office he seeks is the lack of political judgment demonstrated in thinking he could be elected to it, is also happy to join the media-mad by calling the Bush administration "brain dead."[4] He thus affirms that he is a member of the Bush-haters club by tacitly agreeing to treat a proposition he knows not to be true as if it were true.

INTELLIGENCE AND STATUS

And, of course, it's not just any club but a club of the elite: of those who, unlike the stupid president, are smart and show it by commenting on his stupidity. It's just one indication among many of the importance to people these days of claiming the status that goes with high intelligence. "What If Everything You Believed About Investing Was Wrong?" an e-mail from Fisher Investments asked me. I thought I'd heard something like this before, so I tried typing the words "Everything you know about" between quotation marks and ran a Google search on them. This returned 282,000-odd results. Here are just a few of the examples that lead the list,

most of which seem to be titles of books or articles rather
than advertisements:

Everything you know about sex is wrong
Everything you know about love and sex is wrong
Everything you thought you knew about grilling
    is wrong
Everything you know about UI design is wrong
Everything you know about MMOs is wrong
Everything you know about the NBA is wrong
Most everything you know about air pollution
    is wrong
Everything you know about marathons is wrong
Everything you know about abs is wrong
Forget everything you think you know about oil
Everything you know about client security is wrong
Everything you know about video game violence
    is wrong
Everything you know about kids and money is wrong
Everything you know about taxes is wrong
Everything you know about Genesis is wrong
Everything you know about the Web is wrong
Everything you know about the Bush environmental
    record is wrong
What if everything you know about 9/11 is wrong?

Though everything I know about publishing may be wrong
—as the first chapter of Gerry McGovern's and Rob Norton's
book *Content Critical* tells me it is—it can hardly be the case
that I am wrong in thinking that the "Everything is wrong"
formula is vastly overused by publishers and other sellers of

information. I could, as they say, go on. As I was writing this chapter, at least two more books were announced or reviewed with the same formula in their subtitles: "Why everything you know about the game [of baseball] is wrong"[4] and "Everything you think you know about food is wrong."[5] The come-on for the book- or magazine-reader is clearly the promise of information that others do not have and that upsets the notions most people continue to cherish about the matter in question. When this promise sounds most plausible, the result can be such phenomenal bestsellers as Steven Leavitt's and Stephen Dubner's *Freakonomics*, Jared Diamond's *Guns, Germs and Steel*, or Malcolm Gladwell's *Tipping Point* and *Blink*. With such information, available only from the publication you hold in your hand, you will instantly be the proud possessor of a special, higher status than the ruck of those who cling to common knowledge—or even common sense. Not only do these books promise information unavailable anywhere else—or anywhere except for precincts inhabited by specialists in the sort of recondite scholarship which no one but they has time to explore—the import of that information is very possibly, very plausibly, to unlock the hidden secrets of our world.

The marketing of the news is now carried out like the marketing for Fisher Investments. This is yet another example of the media's language of hyperbole which I discussed in the last chapter—and with the same purpose, which is to flatter the reader that he is being invited into the exclusive precincts of a reality inaccessible to those less intelligent than he. Let the common herd go on thinking that they know about sex or food or abs or oil. *You*, dear reader, will know better. You will be given the inside information available only to the smartest players. Or, to put it succinctly, buy a book and become an aristocrat. For knowing what ordinary folk don't know is your ticket to membership in the cognitive elite—which, as Richard Herrnstein and Charles Murray pointed out more than a dozen years ago, is our new aristocracy.[6] A very long time ago, people used to take pride in how honorable they were. More recently, say a century or two ago, that pride was for most people more likely to be invested in goodness or virtue than in honor. One difference between the two was that honor included the idea of being solicitous of one's own honor but virtue, at least in Christian lands, was generally reckoned to include the virtue of humility. Thus, you were less likely to establish your own virtue by moral ostentation than by the denigration of the virtue of others.

Nowadays we seek to be recognized neither for honor nor for virtue but for intelligence. And in the quest to be known as intelligent, some of the traits of honor and virtue have been left as a residue in the crucible of reputation. Among these are a preference for denigrating the intelligence of other people as an indirect way of boasting about one's own. As a claim to status it is so obvious that even a child can emulate it—as the eight-year-old son of the British sociologist Frank Furedi, did when he came home from school one day and announced, "Daddy, I really hate Bush!"

> Until that point, this child had strong views on the subject of football (which he loves), school dinners (which he dislikes) and mobile phones (which he desperately desires). But this was his first statement of political preference. Why did he feel so strongly about the American president?

"Because he's so stupid," my son replied. As a proud father, I would like to boast that my young son and his classmates have developed a precocious interest in political affairs. Unfortunately, that is not the case. Children are no more curious about political life than their elders. Rather, political life in the Western world has become so infantilized that even eight-year-olds can share its brilliant insights.[7]

No doubt the adjective "brilliant" in that passage is intended ironically, but to the mind of an eight-year-old—and to many minds much older—disparaging the intelligence of "Bush" really is a claim to intelligence, an easy way to identify oneself with those who are smart enough to know that the president is dumb.

You'd think that such words lisped by the young Furedi and other political innocents would give the media pause in the eagerness with which they engage in essentially the same kind of status-seeking, but there has been little evidence of it. Perhaps this is because it is in the very nature of journalism for status to be determined by incremental and competitive advances in intelligence—in the other but not unrelated sense of the word as knowledge. Knowing more than someone else, or knowing it first, lies at the very foundation of commercial journalism—as, of course, does the advertising of such claims, however well- or ill-founded. The media have not only vanity but very large financial interests at stake in portraying themselves as being smarter than other people. If they weren't smarter and better informed than you are, for example, why would you pay for access to the fruits of their labors? But the benefit to you of paying is to become smart too, once you have bought the paper or watched or listened to the broadcast and know as much as the journalist who wrote it.

Hence, too, the media's bedrock assumption that the truth is hidden and must be dug out by those with the equipment to do the digging. A corollary of this assumption is that the obvious, instead of being what must be true will tend to become what must *not* be true. The habit of informational status-seeking has schooled us to think that the truth is what's available to the elite, and therefore the truths available to those not of the elite cannot really be true. It can't, for example, be true that the U.S. intelligence services, through a misunderstanding of Arab culture, honestly believed that Saddam Hussein possessed chemical and/or biological weapons and was actively seeking nuclear ones or that President Bush honestly decided to go to war against him at least partly on the basis of what the Director of Central Intelligence at the time, George Tenet, reportedly told him was "a slam-dunk." This would be too obvious. It was what the president claimed and what the stupid people believed. Therefore, if you were smart, you would naturally assume that the obvious was there only to obscure the hidden—and, of course, much more discreditable—motives of the Bush administration for its invasion of Iraq.

SELLING SCANDAL

The belief in the media, echoing that among the political opposition, that "Bush lied" about the weapons of mass destruction became unquestioned fact within a year of the invasion. The reason for this was partly owing to the media's bias towards the Democrats, who were pulled in 2004 by the anti-war left into making similar charges, but it also had to do with the predisposition of the media to seek out scandal as the principal form their highly marketable intelligence about political behavior takes. In the case of the "lies" of the Bush administration, which the Democrats too eagerly took up during the election campaign of 2004, the casting of opposition to the administration in moral rather than practical terms probably cost them the election—since voters were asked to believe that the president was a bad man and not just a mistaken one, which didn't square with ordinary perceptions.

But, of course, if you have taught yourself to believe that you have caught the powerful out in lying it's hard not to make an issue of the fact. The media's willingness to believe in presidential lying has much to do with two of the founding myths of the contemporary media culture: Vietnam and Watergate. Both fit perfectly the paradigm of officials covering up what it then became the job of the media to expose. Again and again Vietnam and Watergate are held up as examples not only of the media's heroism in saving the republic from criminal—or criminally stupid—elected leaders but also as the justification for thinking themselves, as by now they have got into the habit of doing, intellectually and morally superior to those leaders.

In Chapter Two, I noted the importance for the media of being able to represent themselves as lifting the veil of bland and inoffensive appearances, political ones especially, and showing what lies behind it—what politicians would wish to keep hidden and what therefore must be to their discredit. This model of "reality," therefore, consists of the façade put up to deceive people and, behind it, the sordid, corrupt, hypocritical, or otherwise discreditable reality that they have sought to hide and that it is the media's *raison d'être* to expose. It will be observed that this model is designed to make life for the media into one long hunt for scandal— which is in fact what it has become. The Mark Foley scandal of the autumn of 2006 showed us that scandal has become so much a part of our lives, so much in demand by the media eager to turn it into a marketable commodity, that it is now even scandalous for the potential victims of scandal to wish to avoid a scandal.[8]

Within living memory, it would have been thought not only in the congressman's best interests but in everyone else's as well for such a matter to be kept from the public, and for him to resign quietly "for personal reasons." But now the only interests that the media feel obliged to consider are their own, and they stand to gain from airing as much dirty linen in public as possible. The pretense that this is done in the public interest must be kept up, but neither can it be quite hidden that it is, at a minimum, also very much in the media's interest—and, in the Foley case, in that of the political party they overwhelmingly back. Coincidence? You be the judge!

When it becomes the role of the media to find out what is hidden and bring it to light, then anything not hidden is diminished in importance. Politicians have long since recognized this fact of media life, and so it is has become routine for them to "leak" important policy initiatives in advance of their announcement in order to create an artificial sense of excitement about them. The media's assumption that it is the job of government to hide things and their job to find them out thus allows them to cooperate in the charade by which even those things supposedly creditable to the government are hidden from the public so that the media can triumphantly expose them to the world like a magician displaying the rabbit or the quarter or the hard-boiled egg that he himself has hidden. Scandal and hype therefore become much more than any individual case of wrongdoing or the hyperbole with which it is blown out of proportion. They become a way of media life. Media "reality" becomes virtually identical with the presumptive wrongdoing of those in public life, whose attempts to deny or keep hidden such discreditable "realities" about themselves are only further evidence for those realities.

This is also what creates the well-known herd or pack instinct among journalists: nobody wants to be the last to recognize a "reality" whose obviousness by that point means that it has ceased to be reality. In other words, the news is not just subject to fashion, it is like fashion itself in being a wasting asset. The more it becomes the property of those who are not fashionable, the less fashionable it becomes. A naïve observer might almost think you could define "reality" as that which is *not* subject to fashion, but in the media world realities cease to be real when they cease to be fashionable. That was the point made by Walter Kirn when he reviewed Harvey Mansfield's book, *Manliness*, in *The New York Times Book Review* by noting that such a subject could not be taken seriously since the word "manly" was "poignantly out of date ... among even minimally hip Americans."[7] The idea of the "minimally hip" is a happy one and probably perfectly describes the *Times*'s attitude towards its readers. This venerable newspaper might once have been ashamed to publish such a fatuous opinion masquerading as a "review" of a serious work of political philosophy. But living in the world of hip-hype you tend to forget that there can be any reality apart from it. The vanity of those who imagine that it has been given to them to know "reality"—and that reality is easily known—is a cognitively incapacitating ailment that shows up in them only in their attribution of it to others. For of course anyone who, like President Bush, remains stubbornly unwilling to recognize these supposed realities can expect nothing but merciless ridicule for their stupidity, blindness, or even insanity by those whose status among their peers depends on such recognition.

On the Need for Explainers

There was no Google thirty or forty years ago, but I imagine that if there had been you could have obtained a similar result to the one mentioned above by typing in "What makes x tick?" or "What makes x run?" The craze for such formulations tells us something about the journalistic culture that produced them. In the 1960s, when America's romance with psychotherapy was in a state of near-infatuation, a similar excitement could be generated by the promise of *explanation*, usually in psychological terms, of everything from the newest celebrity or political candidate—these were not at the time the same thing—to war, racism, or the inner-city crime rate. What made more or less everything tick was the clockwork mechanism of psychological trauma and the various sorts of responses (aggressive, defensive, compensatory, etc.) that it was thought to elicit. Eventually, people began to get the idea that such explanations did not explain very much since, for one thing, everyone had such or similar traumas and, for another, the same stimuli could produce widely varying responses. But the illusion of explanation was too congenial to be abandoned in a society whose steady progress towards ever more pervasive sorts of meritocracy was accelerating.

Some of these fossilized explanations have since become journalistic memes—as for instance that poverty causes violence—to be taken for granted and employed as the occasion demands. But in general the more lasting consequence of the vogue for explanation has been the assumption that the world demands explanation. It cannot, that is, be what everyone can see it is. Or at least not just that. It hides its true meanings and causes from us, and so creates a need for those who know its ways and can uncover what is hidden. The one assumption on which the power of knowledge to confer status depended was that it had to be of things that those who stood outside the knowing elites did not or could not know. If it was obvious to all, it could not be valuable knowledge. And then, as the media's competition to dispense the kind of knowledge that *was* valuable grew more intense, it began to seem as if what was obvious could not even be true. Certainly it wasn't for the conspiracy theorists who long ago began to proliferate among the ruins of our shared cultural assumptions.

Conspiracy theory, however, is only a vulgarization of what is by now routinely going on at the highest cultural and intellectual levels—and for the same reason, namely that people want to appear intelligent in the eyes of others. The cheapest and easiest way to appear intelligent is to claim to be the possessor of knowledge that is not obvious and so is beyond the capacities of those ordinary folk who judge things by appearances. It ought not to be necessary to point it out, but sometimes appearances and realities do coincide. Sometimes—we might almost say most of the time—what *seems* is also what *is*, though we are more and more inclined to forget this. Those who see their social status as depending on the possession of knowledge unavailable to those lower down in the hierarchy have no use at all for such dull obviousness and are therefore easy prey for the media's offers of access to hidden realities. This is one reason why the media's coverage of politics today is dominated by scandal-hunting of one sort or another, since powerful people may be relied upon to try to keep hidden information that is to their discredit.

I'll come back to this subject in a moment, but at a more sophisticated level even the most exigent policy decisions can be given a quasi-scandalous dimension by hints—and sometimes open speculation—about the real motivations behind them. *Reality*, as usual, is believed to certify itself as such primarily by the twin criteria of being hidden and being, more or less, discreditable—or else why would it be hidden? Today, for example, the war in Iraq is routinely "explained" in terms of everything from "oil"—elaborate at will as to whether this means the administration's serving the interests of the big oil companies out of a corrupt self-interest (more discreditable) or just its slavish service to America's appetite for cheap oil supplies (less discreditable)—to the malign influence of "the "Israel lobby" or Halliburton. Those of a conspiratorial bent will see it as a pretext for the establishment of a police state or a theocracy—or a theocratic police state—while amateur psychologists will cite an Oedipal (or possibly anti-Oedipal) urge on the part of President

Bush to right the wrongs of—or done to—his father. That none of these things have been mentioned by the president himself, or anyone in his administration, only makes them more plausible to the aspirational cognitive elite for whom reality is by definition something hidden and discreditable.

For such people, the only thing that the war couldn't be is what the administration says it is—an attempt to defeat terrorism and terrorists by deposing a tyrant and establishing in his place a functioning democracy in the Middle East. The idea might seem quixotic enough to an ordinary intelligence or naïve judgers-by-appearance. But quixotism is not, to those afflicted with media madness, a dark enough explanation. Beneath such apparent idealism there lurks, for those with sufficient intelligence or guile to see it, one or more of the corrupt and vicious sources always to be found for the acquisition and exercise of power. Simple folks might cling to a belief in the war as an attempt by an ordinarily decent and patriotic president with his country's best interests at heart to further those interests and avenge the grievous wound of 9/11 by making an example of one of America's enemies who was also a sponsor of terrorism. Media sophisticates know that it cannot be that *by definition*.

SCANDAL MANIA BLINDS US TO REAL POLITICAL ERROR AND WRONGDOING

Just suppose that it were true that, to the Bush administration, the operative consideration in deciding to go to war in Iraq really was a sincere belief that America's interests could not but be served by the liberation of those whom this tyrant had oppressed, and the conferring on them of the benefits of American-style democracy. Would not, then, that naïve belief in the capacity of America's armed forces to impose such a democracy on a tribal culture like Iraq's be quite scandalous enough? We might almost say, as Talleyrand did of the murder of the Duc d'Enghien by Napoleon, that it was worse than a crime, it was a blunder. But because the blunder wasn't hidden and it wasn't as discreditable as a hidden motive would have been—for wouldn't we all have liked similarly to hope and believe that Iraq could be transformed into Italy, or Syria into Sweden, by the removal of a few nasty thugs at the top?—it was more or less invisible to those afflicted with media madness, who could only see the professed reasons for the war as a smokescreen for the imaginary and surely much more discreditable "reality" that must lie beneath them.

That's how it came to be that so many from America's intellectual elites set off in pursuit of the will-o'-the-wisp of Bushite mendacity, viciousness, corruption, and, with luck, criminality—for these were things that could only be unmasked with the help of a cleverness like their own—when they might instead have attended to the more obvious failure that was staring them (and, of course, those much less clever than they) in the face. That President Bush was constantly criticized for the wrong things—and in a way that could not but make any man conscious, as he must have been, of his own good faith angrily defensive—made it much less possible to do anything to put that mistake right. While the media have been desperately trying to unearth the scandals that they know must be there and throwing up nothing but such pathetic apologies for high crimes and misdemeanors as the Libby perjury case or attempted sensationalism about the exposure of such routine security measures as the NSA wiretaps—or wireless taps—of phone calls out of the country or the monitoring of bank records, more substantive questions about the war on terror and the war in Iraq have often been ignored.

These questions, you might think it hardly necessary to add, are difficult, even agonizing ones. But the media and, increasingly the political opposition as well, are more interested in the easy answers implied by the assumption of the president's personal stupidity or viciousness. When, for example, the newly elected Senator James Webb of Virginia replied to the State of the Union Address in January of 2007 in the first flush of excitement with the Democrats' recapture of Congress the previous November, he had not a single alternative proposal to mention as a counter to the president's policy of increasing American troop strength in Iraq —not even the withdrawal of the troops which on other occasions he had seemed to favor. He thought it enough of an answer to say that he and other Democrats had foreseen the disaster that most Americans now thought the war in Iraq had become. In other words, they were smarter than the president. That was assumed to be enough, in itself, to determine their fitness and the president's unfitness for office. Politics for Senator Webb was not primarily a matter of *doing* things. Rather, it was an intelligence test: who was better able to foresee and avoid dangers rather than who was more resolute and determined in combating them when they came.

We might note that it is not difficult for the leaders of a superpower like the United States to avoid dangers if avoiding dangers is all that is required of them in the short term— by which I mean an officeholder's term between elections.

The dangers of Islamic terrorism built up through eight years of the Clinton administration when nothing that carried any political cost was ever done about them. That this amounted to Mr. Clinton's kicking the problem down the road for his successor to deal with did not seem matter for scandal to the media. On the contrary, when ABC attempted to show a mini-series called "The Path to 9/11" in September of 2006, the scandal became the filmmakers' for daring to hint that dangers manifest during the Clinton years ought to have been responded to and not just foreseen—indeed, that foreseeing them ought to have involved an effort to forestall them by proactive as well as reactive response. Because action, and especially military action, almost inevitably involves failures and mistakes—failures and mistakes which those who are on the hunt for them may plausibly represent as scandal —any president wishing to keep on the good side of the media would be well-advised to do as little as possible.

Not that Mr. Clinton did not have his own problems with scandal, but, as in Mr. Bush's case, the scandal was irrelevant —indeed, quite spectacularly irrelevant—to the real political, military, and diplomatic failures that a responsible media and opposition ought to have been highlighting. But the political culture must naturally adjust itself to the media culture in an age of scandal. Particularly in America, where political journalists overwhelmingly favor one party over the other, it would take an enormous degree of character and integrity on the part of the favored party, the Democrats, not to abandon proper politics altogether and just sit back, as they have done, and take advantage of the media's endless spinning of scandal against the opposition. The media have made it too easy for the Democrats to make what ought to be the illegitimate case in a democracy that the other side do not just have bad policies but are also bad men. Senator Webb, for example, was elected with the help of what ought to be seen as a textbook case of media scandal-mongering for partisan purposes. His opponent, the Republican incumbent Senator George Allen, was not so subtly portrayed as a racist in *The Washington Post*—the local daily paper for a substantial portion of the electorate in Northern Virginia—for months before the election, and he was happy to reaps the political benefit of this smear.[10]

Even at the time, in the midst of the campaign, John F. Harris, then a writer for the *Post*, could see what was going on. "Cumulatively, the stories highlight a new brand of politics in which nearly any revelation in the news becomes a weapon or shield in the daily partisan wars, and the aim of candidates and their operatives is not so much to win an argument as to brand opponents as fundamentally unfit."[11] He attributed this behavior to the politicians and the new media without noting the extent to which they have obviously learned it from the *Post* and other old media. Martin Kettle, a columnist for *The Guardian* newspaper in London, once called it "punk journalism"—which, he said, "smacks of something bordering on journalistic fascism, in which all elected politicians are contemptible, all judges are disreputable, and only journalists are capable of telling the truth, even though what passes for truth is sometimes little more than prejudice unsupported by facts."[12] But it is, perhaps, what you should expect from those whose livelihoods depend on their continuing to uphold the pretense that they are (a) objective and (b) more intelligent than those who are not—whom they scorn as "partisans."

5 | The Therapeutic Model: Root Causes, Vicious Circles, and Moral Equivalence

WRITING IN 2004 in bitter indignation at the failure of the Bush administration to prevent the terror attacks of September 11, 2001, and its subsequent refusal to accept what he regarded as a sufficient share of blame for this failure, the *Washington Post* columnist Richard Cohen complained:

> Sandy Berger, the national security adviser under Bill Clinton, had told Condi Rice, the national security adviser under George W. Bush, that terrorism would be her No. 1 concern—and yet almost 3,000 lives were lost and a gash punched into the Pentagon and a hole left in the bottom of Manhattan Island. For this, somehow, *no one is at fault.*[1]

I'm prepared to accept that this was a mere inadvertence—that Mr. Cohen did not *really* believe, as it would seem he believes in this passage, that the terrorists were not at fault for their own acts of terrorism. Yet so natural is it for him to think in terms of the hidden causes of things, the causes known only to people like himself, people with inside knowledge of, say, what Sandy Berger told Condi Rice, that he has for the moment forgotten there is any other kind. Yes, yes, his swift and sophisticated mental processes might acknowledge, everyone knows that terrorists are to blame. But my job as a pundit and a columnist is to concern myself with what everyone *doesn't* know—what, in fact, it takes clever people like me to know—namely, the hidden origins of such dire contingencies as 9/11 in the faulty policies of those who, as we suppose, are charged with preventing them. In theory, if we have enough of this superior kind of knowledge we should be able—and we should have been able—to prevent bad things from *ever* happening.

Mr. Cohen is, in short, a closet utopian. Stricken with media madness, he starts from a baseline of perfection and sees any deviation from it as prima facie evidence of wrong-doing and scandal: either incompetence or corruption or both. Keeping anything bad from happening to the American people may not be among the enumerated duties of the president under the Constitution, but the media, especially, find it convenient to treat it as if it were because the assumption vastly increases the potentiality for wrongdoing among politicians—since bad things are always happening—and therefore of opportunities for scandal mongering. Thus, the second-guessing of those in power is the media's favorite sport. And, with the endless recriminations over the war in Iraq, this second-guessing has now spread well beyond the media as an easy and costless way for the intellectually upwardly mobile to demonstrate their superior intelligence in comparison with the unworthy political hacks who more or less illegitimately exercise authority over their country.

As we noticed in the last chapter, this habit of thought is essentially a form of status-seeking, but its impact on American political life and culture has been devastating. Unless they are very thick-skinned indeed—and, say what you like about him, President Bush must be among the most pachy-dermatous of presidents—politicians will spend more and more of their time simply trying not to make mistakes, sweeping potential dangers under the carpet, instead of dealing with them forthrightly, while trying to avoid responsibility for anything that goes wrong. It later happened that Mr. Berger, cited above by Richard Cohen as the very model of executive sagacity, was convicted of illegally removing and destroying files relevant to his years as National Security Adviser from the National Archives for purposes unknown but pretty obviously (it seems to me) related to a similar assumption. For if some mistake of his could, unmade, have prevented these or other terror attacks, then he could only expect that the media and the political opposition would hold him to have been at fault in those attacks if the information ever leaked. The lynx-eyed champions of perfection have created something close to political paralysis.

Intelligence and the Search for Root Causes

It's not only terrorism that has hidden causes. All kinds of behavior that might once have been described as simply wicked are now deemed to have obscure origins that the media see it as part of their job to bring to light. These "root causes" of the world's problems are typically unaddressed by the less intelligent—including most practical politicians —who are more wedded to appearances. When revealed, they also become further proofs of the media's moral and intellectual superiority. "Violence" in particular, is something that always has root causes. So also do crime, poverty, and ignorance, among other things. It is important to remember that the root causes must not be obvious. Otherwise, there is no special role for the media in bringing them to the public's attention. Ignorance, for instance, as a result of poor schooling, cannot be caused by the poor schooling itself, which would be the obvious cause. No, the poor schooling must itself have a less visible cause that, in effect, exonerates the educators who are doing such a poor job.

And here we see the usefulness of being able to shift around root causes as the occasion demands. Crime, for instance, can be a root cause of poverty at the same time that poverty is the root cause of crime. Both are the root causes of ignorance, which in turn is a root cause of both of them. The media never seem to notice this kind of circular reasoning because of the way they tell their stories. A particular criminal incident, for example, can be quite easy to explain in terms of the poverty or ignorance that supposedly caused it. But if the story is about a particular instance of poverty or ignorance instead—say the inability of a high school student to read—then that is a different story, and its cause can be confidently assigned to the rampant crime in and around the school where the student failed to learn to read. If the two stories are told by the same reporter on different days, no one ever supposes that there is any contradiction between them. A root cause one day can become an effect the next and vice versa.

If the unsatisfactoriness of this explanation ever comes to their attention, the media will reply that it is a vicious circle. But this is a mixing of metaphors. A circle cannot have a root; a root cannot also be a circle. If a thing can have roots when required and then metamorphose into a circle, we are right to be suspicious as to whether these explanations are actually explaining anything. In fact, it may seem that they are more obfuscatory than explanatory, and this may have something to do with the fact that the media, like some politicians, have a vested interest in the intractability of many of the problems they write and broadcast about. Root causes become things that, as a practical matter, will never be rooted out and vicious circles things that will never end—though that doesn't mean that politicians cannot be blamed for failing to root them out or those who are caught up in them for failing end them.

This intractability is often an artifact of the explanation for it. I believe, for instance, that it would be relatively easy to get rid of failing schools and give all children a decent primary and even secondary education. It could be done in very short order if all you did was clear out the incompetent and ineffectual teachers and administrators who are consuming public resources to no purpose and give their replacements the necessary moral and legal as well as educational tools to do the job properly. Among these would be the right of individual teachers or administrators to discipline pupils by any means they chose, including physical punishment. But because of the assumption of the self-protective educational establishment, backed up the media, that instead you have to deal with root causes and vicious cycles and eliminate poverty and violence first, the schools can go on failing year after year and the blame will only fall, if it falls on anybody, on the politicians who have failed to deliver on their occasional and sporadic but essentially utopian promises to clean them up.

There is an amazing naïveté in believing these utopian

promises in the first place, but media madness assists in fostering such a belief by its attachment to the chimera of root causes and vicious circles. For if these things function, as they so often do, as an apology for failure in lesser enterprises than bringing about a state of earthly perfection, it follows that nothing can be done until everything can be done. Failing schools must await the millennium in which poverty and crime shall have been eliminated if they are to cease failing. In the meantime, what can we expect but that they will continue to fail? Belief in root causes and vicious circles is also what allows the media to avoid any consideration of the disaster of de-colonization in many parts of the world. If Africa is an appalling mess of poverty, disease, corruption, civil war, and mindless slaughter since the European colonialists left, it becomes very easy for the root-causist to say that this must be because the European colonialists were there in the first place—and that means that, again, nothing can be done short of a utopian transformation, since the European colonialists will always have been there. They, of course, have their guilt to keep them content with washing their hands of the place, but the poor Africans are left to their miseries while media multiculturalists, committed to the assumptions of equality between cultures and peoples, never have to look in the face the real consequences of cultural differences.

It will be observed that this habit of the American media mind makes it natural to assume, as Richard Cohen does in the example that introduced this chapter, that attacks on America must be, somehow, America's fault. That's why so much of the first impulse of the media after 9/11 was to agonize over the question, "Why do they hate us?" Rather than going to war against terrorists and terrorism, said Andy

Rooney on "60 Minutes," it "might be better if we figured out how to behave as a nation in a way that wouldn't make so many people in the world want to kill us." Naturally, our solicitude for the sensibilities of our would-be enemies becomes self-reinforcing, as they learn to appeal to it. Thus, when Her Majesty the Queen saw fit to bestow a knighthood on the novelist Salman Rushdie in June of 2007, the religious affairs minister of Pakistan (and son of the country's late President Zia-ul-Haq), Mohammad Ejaz-ul-Haq, was quoted as saying that "The West always wonders about the root cause of terrorism. Such actions are the root cause of it."[2] As Abraham Lincoln said of the Southern threat to secede if a Republican president were elected, "That is cool. A highwayman holds a pistol to my ear, and mutters through his teeth, 'Stand and deliver, or I shall kill you—and then you will be a murderer!'" But such absurdity doesn't faze our intellectual sophisticates of today. Whatever ill fortune befalls us, it must be because of something we're doing to provoke those whom only the unsophisticated could suppose have themselves caused it. Therefore, all we have to do is find out what it is and stop doing it.

Thus, too, it has become an article of faith for the anti-Iraq war party to believe that it is our efforts to fight Islamicist terrorists in that country that are themselves causing the numbers of terrorists to grow. That used to be known as defeatism, but now it is almost a truism. Doubtless it *is* true that many young Iraqis have been inspired by the Western presence in their country to join the insurgency, or al-Qaeda, but rallying against a perceived enemy is something that happens in all wars. It doesn't mean that we can choose, at this point, not to be the enemy anymore by folding our tents and going home. The media-mad want to believe that we can, however, because of their utopianism. The prevention of terrorism like almost any other sort of evil must be believed to be within our own control—not by combating it but by so clever and sagacious a mix of policy as to forestall it. Indeed, it often seems that very little cleverness or sagacity is required, and that it would be quite a simple matter to end these evils but for the bungling of the boobs in power who lack the imagination or intellect to address root causes.

How Easy to Exit the Cycle of Violence

Where problems are so intractable as to qualify as vicious circles, their solutions are still widely supposed to be in the control of those who are caught up in them if only they have the wisdom to opt out. This is especially true of that most terrible of vicious circles: "the cycle of violence." The subtext, for example, of most media reports from the war in Iraq—from the ones on how it is putting a strain on the capabilities of the National Guard or adversely affecting recruitment efforts at home to the ones on how the American presence there has led to the radicalization of this or that faction or opportunities for Iranian subversion—is that America has an easy option for the avoidance of these and other evils in simply choosing not to be involved any longer in the struggle there. The entirety of Democratic policy towards the war at the time of writing is built on the same assumption, even where there is a tacit realization that no such option exists.

Rhetorically, if not practically, the media have made it almost a condition of being taken seriously on matters of war and peace that we adopt the utopian viewpoint of those who engage in "peace studies" that by refusing to defend ourselves—and so opting out of the "cycle of violence"—we will make self-defense unnecessary. Where does such a curious notion come from? I think it is from the long-term influence on American culture of the psychotherapeutic movement. A few years ago, a *New Yorker* cartoon by Bruce Eric Kaplan showed two ducks sitting on a reed-fringed pond. One was saying to the other: "Maybe you should ask yourself why you're inviting all this duck hunting into your life right now." The foundational therapeutic assumption that our problems are in our own control, whatever may or may not be its justification for those in therapy, is about as useful to political leaders as it is to ducks, but at least it has the merit of providing the media with still more opportunities for questioning the intelligence or the probity of the politicians whom they see it as their business to criticize, ridicule, or humiliate.

There are similar assumptions behind the "moral equivalence" argument that was so popular during the Cold War and that has since been revived in some quarters to characterize what once was called the War on Terrorism, then, briefly, the Long War, but what now, apparently, has no name at all. In theory, the Bush administration's religiosity, for example, is no better and no worse than the religious fanaticism of Osama bin Laden, but in practice those who hold this view quite often come to think that President Bush is actually much worse than the world's most famous troglodyte. They can be observed at anti-war rallies holding up photos of the president and vice president labeled "The *Real* Terrorists." Shortly before she left the ABC talk show, "The View," in mid-2007, Rosie O'Donnell gave voice to a similar opinion—though she later attempted to draw back from it by saying (or implying) that she had not meant to imply what she plainly did mean to imply—when she said that "655,000 Iraqi civilians are dead. Who are the terrorists? . . . I'm saying if you were in Iraq, and the other country, the United States, the richest in the world, invaded your country and killed 655,000 of your citizens, what would you call us?"[3]

Never mind that of the number of Iraqis killed since the American invasion—almost certainly very much lower than Miss O'Donnell's number—the vast majority have been killed not by the United States but by their fellow Iraqis. Her point of view would not make even the minimal sense it does without the assumption that our own leaders are willfully refusing to end what it must lie within their power to end—and that the jihadis, like the Soviets before them, must have no such powers of forbearance towards our provocations of them. Such are the origins, or the root causes if you will, of what the late Jeane Kirkpatrick called the "Blame America First" party. Except that, once this kind of thinking has become a habit, it is apparently easy to forget that the terrorist attackers bear *any* responsibility for their own actions. Blame America First becomes Blame America Only. And not only America's leaders either. In an extreme example of media madness, one that out-Baudrillarded Jean Baudrillard, Ward Churchill won for himself something of a following for saying that the victims of the attacks on the World Trade Center had been "little Eichmanns" who only got what was coming to them.

Not that the media themselves could believe anything so outrageous, but outrageousness obviously makes for better copy and more colorful characters than calmer and more judicious analyses. Besides, the demands of "objectivity" require that even the most outrageous or idiosyncratic viewpoints be treated with a respect equal to that accorded the most judicious and commonly held—except that the commonly held may be treated with *less* respect precisely on the grounds that it is common and not due to the intellection of the media and cultural elites. No enemy of America is so bad that some among the media-mad of America will not excuse him on the grounds that he was provoked by America in the first place. Hugo Chavez? "I want to see—say one thing about him," said Nina Totenberg of National Public Radio. "He is the class clown, but we have made him. We should have ignored him long ago." Mahmoud Ahmadinejad? The talk-show host Bill Maher put him and Mr. Chavez together: "Even though these guys are bad in a lot of ways, it is also true that the substance of what they said—that the U.S. is a bully, that we want to rule the world with threats and bombs, that we're imperialistic—what I thought was, you know, this is a speech I've heard over the years many times by tin horn dictators at the U.N. against the U.S. It's just that now it strikes a lot of people as true."[4]

MORAL EQUIVALENCE AS A LIBERAL AND MULTICULTURAL COMMONPLACE

Over and over again in *The Washington Post* and, especially, *The New York Times*, columnists and pundits have sought to cultivate a reputation for wisdom by pointing to an alleged symmetry between the religious fanaticism of jihadi terrorists and "the religious right" in America long associated with

President George W. Bush.[5] Couldn't they tell any difference between the sponsors of suicide bombings of civilians and those who were trying to stop suicide bombings? Presumably not: because the presumptions of moral equivalence in the mind of the media are too strong. The *reductio ad absurdum* of this presumption, as in Miss O'Donnell's contention that "radical Christianity is just as threatening as radical Islam in a country like America,"[6] is quite easy to ridicule. Some years ago, the satirical magazine *Private Eye* ran a cartoon that portrayed a typical Anglican vicar in his pulpit making his after-service announcements and saying, "And there is a sign-up sheet in the vestry for next week's suicide car-bombing of the Mormons." But the absurdity is no greater than that of the more acceptable face of media gravitas, Bob Schieffer of CBS News, who claimed that for America to put terrorists in secret CIA prisons was tantamount to "adopting the methods of our enemies."[7]

Which methods would those be? Suicide bombing? Hacking off the heads of hostages? If the terrorists ever use secret prisons, it's only to keep their hapless victims until they are murdered. But Mr. Schieffer's attachment to the media truism of moral equivalence has relieved him of the duty of thinking. It is a common affliction. Consider Ted Turner's take on the question of nuclear weapons in Iran. "They're a sovereign state," he told David Letterman in an interview on "The Late Show" in 2006. "We have 28,000. Why can't they have 10? We don't say anything about Israel —they've got 100 of them approximately—or India or Pakistan or Russia. And really, nobody should have them. They aren't usable by any sane person."[8] Obviously to Mr. Turner, these weapons are equally dangerous, irrespective of whom they're pointed at and likely to be used against. It seems not even to occur to him that one nuclear weapon in the hands of an enemy of his country could be a matter of any more concern to its statesmen and generals—and is presumably of less concern, since he thinks the numbers, though mistaken, relevant—than 28,000 in the hands of those charged with fighting against such enemies.

In other words, it becomes a point of pride for the men and women of the media to see themselves as not only without a party but also without a country. The attitude of being, by virtue of being journalists, above and outside of the international conflicts they describe has become characteristic of the American media.

> President Bush and President Mahmoud Ahmadinejad of Iran, separated by several hours and oceans of perspective, clashed at the United Nations on Tuesday over Iran's nuclear ambitions and each other's place in the world. The two leaders bookended a long day of speeches at the opening of the General Assembly, but seemed to speak past each other as European and American diplomats continued the delicate work of setting terms for talks with Iran over its uranium enrichment program.[9]

The New York Times can never let you know that one of these presidents, and one of these perspectives, has—or has ever had—any more claim on the loyalties of the authors than the other. Objectivity, a vain enough conceit even at the micro-

level of internal partisan debate, has now gone megalo-
maniacal, extending even to the abolition of such seemingly
ineradicable aspects of identity as a journalist's nationality.

REPORTING SUB SPECIE AETERNITATIS: THE JOURNALIST AS GOD

This was clear at least as long ago as 1987, when in a panel
discussion, Mike Wallace of "60 Minutes" berated the late
Peter Jennings of ABC News for saying that if he knew
beforehand of an enemy ambush prepared for American
troops he would not regard it as a violation of his journalistic
ethics to warn the Americans. Though a Canadian himself,
Jennings thought that his higher duty would be to the troops.
"You don't have a higher duty. No. No. You're a reporter!"
Mr. Wallace had said, and Jennings regarded himself as
properly chastised. "I chickened out," he later said.[10] By now
the Mike Wallace attitude, shocking enough to some at the
time, has become journalistic second nature. How else to
account for the disingenuous response of Bill Keller, executive editor of *The New York Times* to complaints that his
newspaper had acted unpatriotically in exposing details of
the Bush administration's program of monitoring international banking records as an anti-terrorism measure?

> It's an unusual and powerful thing, this freedom that
> our founders gave to the press. Who are the editors
> of *The New York Times* (or the *Wall Street Journal*,
> *Los Angeles Times*, *Washington Post* and other publi-
> cations that also ran the banking story) to disregard
> the wishes of the President and his appointees? And

yet the people who invented this country saw an aggressive, independent press as a protective measure against the abuse of power in a democracy, and an essential ingredient for self-government. They rejected the idea that it is wise, or patriotic, to always take the President at his word, or to surrender to the government important decisions about what to publish.[11]

That he begs the question of "abuse of power" and poses the false antithesis between publishing the details of national security measures and agreeing "to always take the President at his word" may suggest some lingering twinge of conscience about it, but Mr. Keller is otherwise as far down the road as Mr. Wallace towards recognizing no obligation to his country when his higher obligations as a journalist are in question.

What breach of government or military secrecy *wouldn't* the editors of *The New York Times* publish in the name of a legitimate public interest? The actual battle plan for the invasion of Iraq? Nope, they did that, on the front page nearly nine months before the invasion, after what purported to be the plan was leaked to the paper by a disgruntled Pentagon official:

A spokesman for *The Times* said today that while the newspaper could not discuss the nature of its confidential sources, "we are satisfied that the article we printed on July 5 about contingency planning for action on Iraq was consistent with responsible citizenship. We took appropriate steps to determine that while addressing matters of legitimate public concern, we were not jeopardizing current or prospective military operations," the spokesman said.[12]

In the very earliest days of the insurgency, CBS News featured an interview by its correspondent, David Hawkins, of insurgents who by their own admission had killed American soldiers.[13] No one thought much about it. It was what journalists did—just as, for the sake of "access," they were prepared, as CNN later admitted it had been, to keep from the public much of what they know of Saddam Hussein's tyranny. Nowadays, it isn't even controversial when ABC news reports on America's covert operations inside Iran—information about which operations seems to have come from yet another CIA leak.[14]

It's not just that the media-mad weigh the one loyalty against the other and decide which has the greater claim on them—though journalists make a very brief and unpersuasive show of doing this. It's that they would regard it as a shame to their intellects, or their professionalism, to act according to their country's interests rather than their own. If they are as media-mad as Ted Turner, they might even become unable to understand how their country's interests could be rightfully of any more moral weight to *anybody* than those of any other country. Similarly, Jack Cafferty of CNN's "Situation Room" greeted the government's presentation of evidence that Iran had been providing insurgents in Iraq with ordnance that was being used to kill American soldiers by comparing it to America's supply of weaponry to the *mujahideen* of Afghanistan during the Cold War? "So, that was OK," he said with what he obviously regarded as a trenchant irony, "but it's not OK if Iran—I'm, I'm confused,

Wolf."[15] He doesn't know the half of it! To such people it is hypocritical of us to oppose the actions taken against ourselves by an enemy if we have taken similar actions against an enemy. It's like saying that the British were hypocritical for bombing Berlin because they hadn't much liked it when the Germans were bombing London. In such a world, clearly, war itself would be impossible.

Which is the point. If you start with the assumption that there must always be some neutral third position from which to observe everything, whether it be the opposition of Democrat and Republican or America and the violently anti-American or even of good and evil, it's hard not to end with the assumption that this position is to be recommended to everybody, so clearly is it a more morally advanced position than that of the partisans or patriots who demand that we take one side or the other. It shows that the utopianism and love of moral equivalence of the media-mad ultimately has its origins in the media's pretensions to objectivity, and therefore to an entitlement to a privileged position above the battle and disengaged from the great conflicts of the day, whether political, diplomatic, or military. The media-mad are the class of the classless, the faction of the factionless.

The essential falsity of this position should be more and more clear as the madness extends farther and farther beyond the media themselves to most of the educated class from which they draw their personnel. The enlightened, tolerant, progressive, and generally pacific views of such people—like the freedoms enjoyed by the American or European media—are every bit as thoroughly grounded in Western culture as Christian fundamentalism or the sort of moralizing foreign policy that has been favored by the post-9/11 Bush administration and that our new progressives have only latterly found to be so objectionable. But their Olympian pretensions are a delusion, and the mirror image of the self-righteousness they complain of in avowed partisans and patriots. Their enemies are the same, too, but the progressives and utopians imagine that they can be defeated—or turned into non-enemies—by moral rather than by military superiority. The dangers into which such utopianism is leading us, and has already led us, are the theme of our final chapter.

6 | Conclusion: Helping Celebrities to Bring Utopia

"WAS MADONNA'S Live Earth guitar solo real?" asked Matthew Moore in the London *Daily Telegraph* a few days after the event in question in June of 2007.[1] If so, it was the only thing about Live Earth that was real. A pop music extravaganza taking place in nine venues on seven continents, including Antarctica, Live Earth was the perfect media "event"—which is to say not an event at all but a simulacrum of one called into existence by and unimaginable apart from the media themselves. It may have been, as the impresario and former Vice President Al Gore claimed, "the largest global entertainment event in all of history"—though his claim to an audience of more than two billion people worldwide has more than a whiff of Gore-tesque hyperbole about it—but "entertainment" as well as "event" has to be severely qualified. Clearly, a big part of the entertainment lay in the warm glow of self-satisfaction it afforded the participants, both those on stage and those in the audience, for the support their presence gave to its consciousness- and money-raising on behalf of another media phenomenon, "Global Warming."

I hope it will be understood that when I write about global warming as a media phenomenon I am offering no opinion on the related but quite different subject of whether or not the long-term trend lines for oceanic and atmospheric temperatures are affected by human activities or, if so, whether or not they are likely to produce dire consequences for the world or, if so, how dire they are likely to be or when they are likely to befall us or what can be done about them. I am no more qualified to give an opinion on these subjects than Madonna is. But "Global Warming" as it is understood by her and her fellow celebrities is something quite different. It is an opportunity for them to show that they have the right, socially approved feelings of compassion and concern about this putative matter of global significance. That makes it also an opportunity for the media to indulge their passion for celebrities and celebrity feelings and to market these to a large public. For the members of that public, it is an opportunity to feel that the same creditable feelings become more creditable in them for being shared by the celebrities. Finally, the "event" is also an opportunity for Mr. Gore and the other self-appointed trustees of the alleged Global Warming crisis in the pressure group, the Alliance for Climate Protection, to make money which they can then use to influence real political events, such as elections.

CELEBRITIES AND THE MORALIZATION OF POLITICS

But Live Earth itself was carefully and rather ostentatiously nonpolitical in the way that the media like to see themselves as nonpolitical—that is, with its political agenda disguised by moralism. When Howard Kurtz of *The Washington Post* raised the question of whether NBC's extensive coverage of Live Earth—with its cable affiliates it devoted more than thirty hours to the show—didn't amount to giving the network's imprimatur to a political campaign, Dan Harrison, an NBC senior vice president, told him: "I really don't think climate change is a political issue. . . . Everyone agrees it's happening. If it's a political issue, it's whether the political will exists to address that change. We know we need to do something, and this is a way to heighten awareness."[2] This is also what Al Gore thinks. In the Oscar-winning documentary about him, *An Inconvenient Truth*, he says that the problem of global warming is not a political but a moral issue. So much, then, for "debate" or "controversy."

For, shorn of its political dimension in order to suit the media's "objective" and "nonpartisan" pretense, the global warming question actually becomes much more partisan—and much more intractable. In making it into a moral issue, the Gore team—in alliance with most of the world's celebrities and the media—are insisting that those who don't agree with them are not just misguided or in error but also immoral. The strategy of *An Inconvenient Truth* was like that in the title of Mr. Gore's book about the Bush administration, *The Assault on Reason*—to make any opposition to his views illegitimate, either immoral or irrational. In the film, rather than dealing with such mundane political matters as what, in practical terms, the government that Mr. Gore once aspired to lead could actually do about global warming, or how much it would cost to do it in relation to other national priorities and how much we will all have to give up in return for how much benefit in terms of lower aggregate temperatures after ten, fifty, or a hundred years for each dollar—or each trillion dollars—spent, he simply showed a cute graphic of an old fashioned balance-scale with the earth on one side and a pile of gold bars on the other. Is any amount of money, the film asks, worth the destruction of the earth as we know it?

But of course the destruction of the earth as we know it is like the destruction of America as we know it—which, according to Democratic fundraiser Al Gore, is what President Bush has lately accomplished on the domestic front.[3] Both, that is, are eensy-weensy overstatements and both have the same purpose, which is to take advantage of the scandal-obsessed media's already strong suspicion that everything which was once thought of as a political issue is really a moral issue. Nor is it any accident that the former vice president and the media are both star-struck. A moralized political arena is in nobody's interests except the media's and that of the ever-swelling ranks of the celebrities who need to validate themselves by demonstrating their "compassion" or "concern" about world problems so big that, like poverty or climate change, they cannot be expected personally to do anything about them except to sing songs and make gestures that show how much they care.

In the last two or three decades, and especially since the end of the Cold War, the celebrity culture has gone mainstream. Maureen Orth, who now writes for *Vanity Fair*, noted that in 1977 it took her two days to persuade her editors at *Newsweek* to let her cover the funeral of Elvis Presley. And even though she broke the story that Presley had died of an overdose and not, as had been officially given out, a heart attack, *Newsweek*'s cover that week was on Jimmy Carter's budget director, Bert Lance, who had escaped indictment. "It was inconceivable in those days," she observes, "that the death of a show business icon could bump off even a second-rate White House story."[4] *The New York Times* devoted a single paragraph to Presley's death. Compare that to the orgy of coverage that the respectable media, including *The New York Times* and *Newsweek*, devoted thirty years later to the demise of Anna Nicole Smith, a celebrity whose accomplishments were, to put it charitably, very much less impressive even in pop cultural terms than Elvis Presley's.

It is not just the media but the culture which has changed. People who, thirty years ago, would have been ashamed to admit to an interest in the lives and loves of such a person as Anna Nicole Smith, if they had had one, are ashamed no more. A whole new branch of the media has come into existence since 1974 when *People* magazine led the way up-market for celebrity gossip and tittle-tattle. Thirty years later, the median household income of readers of *Us Weekly* was $77,967. At first, bad taste and vulgarity became funny; then they became simply acceptable, even to the social elites. In part, at least, this was owing to the moral shake-up that produced the celebrity culture in the first place. The logic of that culture insisted on the denial that anyone was better than anyone else. If celebrities were "just like us" it meant that we were just like them, and that we had no standing to set ourselves up as being better than they were for not taking an interest in the sordid details of their personal lives.

As Emma Chastain put it in *The New Republic* online, "*Us* doesn't condemn the drug addicts, philanderers, pornographers, anorexics, shoplifters, and wife beaters it chronicles. It frets over the damage to their careers, roots for them, hopes they'll pull themselves together. With its liberal and forgiving attitude, *Us* allows readers to slum without feeling that they are slumming."[5] But this same moral laxity with respect to their private lives has come to be balanced with a cloying moralism when it comes to their pronouncements on matters of public interest. The celebrity "narrative," as we might say, is one of someone who has all the usual range of human failings and maybe some to spare, all of which we expect to take an interest in, but whose heart—those feelings for which the media is always on the lookout in order to sell us a false sense of intimacy with the world's newsmakers— is indisputably in the right place.

THE MEDIA'S INTEREST IN MORALIZING POLITICS

In June of 2007, a couple of weeks before Madonna strummed (or didn't strum) her guitar at Wembley on behalf of a cooler world, the BBC issued an eighty-one-page report titled *From Seesaw to Wagon Wheel*, which contained the results of a year-long internal investigation into the question of bias at the state-sponsored broadcasting corporation. In Britain, everyone who owns a television set is required by statute to pay an annual fee of over $250 to cover the costs of the BBC's programming, so it is obviously a matter of some concern to the corporation's trustees—to say nothing of the politicians who have mandated its public support—to address the charges of bias and partisanship which have grown increasingly insistent in recent years. And, lo, the report came clean! The BBC *was* biased, it said—institutionally so. It was a fair cop. So it seemed that we media watchdogs had got them bang to rights.

Uh, not so much. On closer inspection the report was just another one of those ombudsman's columns that acknowledges a small fault—perhaps we went a little too far here or there—in order to demonstrate the good faith necessary to deny a larger fault. The report's examples of bias were few and poor and bore little or no resemblance to those most often cited by the corporation's critics. It said nothing, for example, about the BBC culture's pervasive anti-Americanism, which many had complained of, nor of its scarcely hidden antagonisms towards the Bush administration, the Iraq war, and the state of Israel, also frequently mentioned by its critics. On no matter of genuine partisan contention was the BBC prepared to admit to taking one side or another. No, the bias to which the BBC was prepared to admit was being overzealous in its support of such presumptively good causes as Sir Bob Geldof's Live Aid and Live 8 campaigns, or the "Make Poverty History" effort of 2005. Only those churlish enough to deny that these were, in fact, good causes would be likely to think that such a bias as this was any great matter for concern.

Accordingly, the institutional reprimand made no discernible difference to the eagerness with which the BBC rushed to give its imprimatur to Live Earth. "When pop stars assemble to save the world, an order goes out from White City," wrote Michael Henderson in the *Daily Telegraph* of the BBC's London headquarters, "as if from Caesar Augustus: all roads lead to north London."[6] Forget, for the moment, the much more serious instances of bias which this one is meant to obscure. The media's support of such celebrity intrusions into the political or quasi-political as Live Earth or Make Poverty History is symptomatic of a much more serious sort of corruption than even the most blatant if still unacknowledged preference given to one side over another in a legitimate political debate. For attempts to mobilize the masses on behalf of ending poverty or preventing global warming are, among other things, also attempts to short-circuit political debate by a moralization of political conflicts which, if they are to be resolved in any helpful way, must not be moralized.

Mr. Henderson of the *Telegraph* traces it all back to the late John Lennon, "that bullying, cowardly, sentimental Liverpudlian. He had to turn himself into a human sandwich-board, proclaiming 'All You Need Is Love' and 'Power to the People' and other slogans. No wonder [the satirical magazine] *Private Eye* based its all-purpose pop buffoon, Spiggy Topes ('Love Is Good, Hate Isn't'), on that hollow man."[7] It's not the usual view either of John Lennon or of pop musicians out to save the world, but neither is the absurdity it makes fun of quite unrecognizable in Live Earth and similar ventures. "Love Is Good, Hate Isn't" doesn't take the pop cultural sensibility all that much further in the direction of absurdity than the real-life interview question of Ann Curry to Trudie Styler, wife of the pop musician Sting, during NBC's three hours of prime-time coverage given to Live Earth: "Why do you care so much?" she asked. What answer from the most ignorant or drugged out pop star could be half as fatuous as a question like that from the "objective" American broadcast media?

Not that objectivity matters when it comes to celebrities —which is really the point. The more that politics can be reduced to celebrity or Live Earth terms, that is to manifestations of creditable feelings, the better the media and the politicians seeking to exploit them will like it. By reducing natural matters of controversy to the uncontroversial, they further marginalize genuine political debate and so bring us a step nearer to a world of discourse like the media's, dominated by scandal-hunting on the one hand and celebrity worship on the other. For who, without scandal, could disagree with the proposition that war or racism or global warming or poverty ought to be opposed? Peace is good; war isn't, as the celebrity might say. Therefore, if his branding as a quasi-official opponent of war, or any other bad thing he may care to name, has been confirmed by the media as not the least—or the greatest—of the things for which he is famous, he is free to promote his agenda not on the grounds of its internal coherence, if any, or its likely efficacy but on the simple principle that no decent person could be against it.

Fortunately the celebrities themselves seldom seem to have much in the way of a worked-out agenda. Their engagement with the causes they advocate need only be emotional. Intellectually, they tend to operate at the level of Petra Nemcova, a model whose contribution to Live Earth was to explain what she had learned when, on a photo shoot in Thailand, she had nearly drowned in the tsunami of 2005. "While I was there, I didn't feel hate towards nature," she said. "I felt nature was screaming for help." Any more detailed prescription for such "help," however, could interfere with the opportunities for moral posturing that celebrities seek out by involving themselves with such causes.

Live Earth, like *An Inconvenient Truth*, limited its few actual policy recommendations to things like using lower wattage light-bulbs or driving more fuel-efficient cars. Anything more would have taken it a little too obviously in the direction of the political, rather than the moral, and its real purpose, like that of all causes suitable for celebrity endorsement, is to persuade us that the political has become the moral. It's the same impulse that is at work in a negative way in the media's obsessive interest in scandal. It's not enough for them to oppose someone on the grounds that his policies are faulty or won't produce the desired effect. The myth of objectivity won't allow them to do that in any case. But it will allow them to suggest with more or less subtlety that he ought to be opposed because he is a bad man— perhaps a racist, like Senator Allen, or a liar, polluter, and pander to the rich like President Bush.

CELEBRITY UTOPIANISM

Live Earth notwithstanding, large-scale demonstrations of celebrity concern for anything as vague as poverty or the environment may be a wasting asset. Even Alessandra Stanley, the television critic for *The New York Times*, could not help noticing about Live Earth that "this seven-continent, multimedia eco-extravaganza was colored by the very complacency it vowed to combat: No matter how dire the problem, the solution can be small and painless."

> Celebrity-driven charity concerts always blend good works with smug self-promotion; the camera has a way of letting the air out of the best-intentioned event. Live Earth, however, had an especially precarious balance between eco-consciousness and ego-consciousness. The "think small" sermon was perhaps the only one that could register with a society so unused to sacrifice, but—if only by the event's own carbon-offsetting, enviro-calculations—it seemed a somewhat timid exhortation for such a huge expense

of energy, talent and time. Or perhaps it just seemed too convenient for those celebrating.[8]

There is also a certain dissonance between the apparent ends and the means that, as Neil McCormick put it in the skeptical *Telegraph*, can be "often comically inappropriate, juxtaposing excessive rock acts such as Metallica with films about not over-filling your kettle."[9]

But if people are beginning to become a bit jaded about celebrities' good causes, the celebrity principle by which political questions can only be approached by being moralized is still strongly at work among the same media in which it has become a cliché to criticize President Bush for excessive moralism. The media have become like those demonstrators who hold up the posters on which photos of the president or vice president are labeled "The Real Terrorists."[10] Each form of moralism has become the mirror image of the other—as it almost inevitably will do in this media environment that gives us no other language but the moral in which to discuss matters of war and peace. When the media blame President Bush for excessive moralism, they are really blaming themselves, since it is they who have created the political context in which only the most high-minded moral principles are seen as appropriate to discussions of war and peace. Increasingly, this same moral language is being extended to other political subjects as well with the connivance of the media. This is not only because it gives them far more scope for scandal-hunting, as I discussed in Chapter Four, but also because it is the natural corollary of the utopianism I described in Chapter Five. If you assume that war and peace or fighting poverty and climate change are matters of simple moral choice, you are also assuming that people have far more control over the world's most intractable problems than history gives any warrant for supposing that they actually have.

In the debate over the war in Iraq, for instance, both the media and the Democratic opposition to the Bush administration have come routinely to assume that the political choice to be made is between fighting it and not fighting it. Put that way, the problem naturally leads the media and the opposition to the conclusion that President Bush is either stupid or wicked—or both, though this seems hardly plausible—for choosing to fight rather than not to fight. But no war in history, including this one, can properly be cast in such terms. Or, to put it another way, history shows us no way of choosing not to fight, so long as there is still fight in the enemy, except for surrender. There are some among the opponents of President Bush who are unafraid of this word —the rest prefer, at the time of writing, the rather comical euphemism of "redeployment"—because they think that surrender would only be his surrender and not America's. It is a vain expectation. In the eyes of the world, and especially of America's enemies, it is America which is committed to the struggle, and it will be America—America's will and America's might—which will have failed in it if the anti-war party has its way. That's just the way the world works. Only a utopian could think otherwise.

PRACTICAL UTOPIANISM AND GESTURAL POLITICS

Recently, a *New York Times* music critic characterized this nation's recent history as a growth "from a nation of hungry dreamers fleeing the Depression and fighting 'the good war' into an arrogant empire drunk on power and angry at the failure of the American dream to bring utopia."[11] The casual assumption, so characteristic of media madness, that "utopia" is what the American dream can be faulted for failing to "bring" helps to explain why otherwise serious people are prepared to give so much credence to celebrities and their causes. We may speak jokingly about celebrities wanting to "save the world," but at some level that's just what we expect them to do. Whatever their shortcomings, they keep the hope alive that "utopia" is just a matter of making the right moral choices as they, guided by their publicists, routinely do. The media exploit that hope, even if they do not share it. Like all utopianism, theirs is incapable of compromising without destroying itself. What compromise can there be with perfection even when—especially when—it is only hypothetical?

That hypothetical perfection shadows more and more of what the media "cover," from the Iraq war to health insurance to campaign finance to gun control. More and more frequently media madness leads to the assumption that all these immensely complicated and difficult matters are moral rather than political. The choices they demand of us thus become simple and binary ones: either we are for or against the war, for or against universal health care, for or against limiting the amount of money in politics, for or against getting guns off the street. Putting the questions in this form is a way of pre-determining the answer that people give to them, but it doesn't bring us any closer to real-world solutions to any of the underlying problems. You might almost think that the media aren't interested in real-world solutions. And the symbolic solutions they are interested in can often make things worse, even much worse, without denting the media culture's sublime confidence that, by championing them, they have taken the right side in a moral controversy.

Take campaign finance reform. It is by now painfully obvious not only that the McCain-Feingold law has failed to limit the amount of money in politics, but also that it has helped to make the money that there is in politics significantly less accountable to the political process. Politicians are likely to have to work harder to raise it, which can only increase the extent to which they are beholden to those from whom they do raise it, and those who are not politicians at all but very rich backers of some favorite measure or another have seen the political power of their money increased enormously by being devoted directly to "issue" ads and independent interest groups instead of funneling it through political parties and candidates. The issue ads and pressure groups—including Al Gore's Alliance for Climate Protection, which did so well out of Live Earth—then become further means for the moralization of politics, encouraging the candidates to identify themselves with the "right" symbolic measures rather than seeking practical answers to practical questions.

Yet there is little support anywhere in the media for a reconsideration of McCain-Feingold. Because it was sold in the first place not on the grounds of any practical utility it might have but as The Right Thing To Do, it must always be The Right Thing To Do, even if its practical utility is nil, or less than nil. The same will go for any palliative measures— and the chances of there being any other kind of measures are slim to none—that will eventually be adopted as a result of the great celebrity crusade against Global Warming. The price you pay for engaging in symbolic politics is that your symbols must become sacrosanct. If a prospective "Saving the Planet" bill turns out to be full of measures that will bankrupt nations and immiserate millions, these will have to be—in theory at least—acceptable losses. In practice, of course, it's a different story, as the 95–0 vote in the U.S. Senate against ratification of the Kyoto Accords showed. Any non-suicidal politician will naturally proclaim his Madonna-like love for the planet while sticking pretty close only to the interests of the part of the planet that is eligible to vote for him. But there is a price to be paid for such a comically wide divergence between theory and practice in the impoverishment of political discourse and the further increase of public cynicism about politics and politicians—which also benefits the media, who are their scourges.

Utopians can only continue to be utopians at the cost of some considerable degree of self-deception—or, to use the favorite psychotherapeutic language of the media themselves, "denial." I cannot but be aware of the irony involved in my accusing the media of the same mental infirmity that in Chapter Three of this book I took them to task for accusing President Bush of. In my own defense I can only say that I do not believe that what I am describing is a clinical condition or even analogous to a clinical condition. It is, as I said in my introduction, merely media madness. This is not a new thing. People have been ignoring what they choose not to see since long before psychiatrists appropriated the phenomenon as a form of mental disorder, and there are a plethora of social occasions on which we would think it, rather, a sign of mental disorder *not* to ignore things which, un-ignored, would create scandal, conflict and unnecessary upset to others. As I noted in Chapter Three,[12] these occasions are especially frequent in the lives of political, military, and diplomatic leaders, and to take their avoidance of "reality" on these occasions as evidence of "denial" is to be unpardonably disingenuous in a way that is characteristic of media madness.

The media, however, by purporting only to deal with the alleged realities behind the appearances of public life, are left with no better explanation for their error than self-deception when those "realities" shall have been shown to be nothing of the kind. Every one of the president's pronouncements about the war may eventually be proven to be in error without the fact's casting any aspersion whatsoever either on his sanity or his moral probity, since putting the most hopeful face upon a bad situation is part of the duty of a leader charged with preventing panic and disorderly retreat. For the media's mistakes and misconceptions there is no such excuse. Having nailed their colors to the mast of "truth," the media-mad have no better answer themselves than "denial" if—as in the case of campaign finance above— their truth shall begin to look like falsehood.

CONCLUSION: WILL MEDIA MEGALOMANIA SURVIVE THE MEDIA?

Not that they ever have to resort even to that excuse. For the worst thing about the media culture is that there is nothing or no one that can call it to account. Nor is there any appeal in public life against its judgments. There is no one before whom those afflicted with media madness will defer, no one with the power to make them feel ashamed or overawed or to make them notice when they are wrong and come to terms with their error. Their conceit of themselves, like so many of the policies they advocate, in moral rather than political terms so raises the stakes in our national discourse that everyone becomes trapped in a psychodrama of good and evil. As I said at the outset, we are no longer living in that world and no longer have to live according to its rules, or with its media-mad fantasies of "objectivity" or "realities" which exclude heterogeneous points of view. That liberation is what has produced the flight to the blogosphere and other alternatives to the mainstream. We must simply hope that, happy in our media niches, we won't find that we have taken our media madness with us.

Notes

Introduction

1 Headline to article by Richard Owen and Ruth Gledhill in *The Times* of July 11, 2007 (www.timesonline.co.uk/tol/comment/faith/article2056 515.ece). See also "Vatican Reaffirms Catholic Primacy," the Reuters story by Phil Stewart as published in *The Washington Post* of July 11, 2007 (www.washingtonpost.com/wp-dyn/content/article/2007/07/10/AR2007071000395.html)

2 The title of his book (New York: Free Press, 2007).

3 New York: Encounter Books, 2006.

Chapter One

1 "According to the *New York Times*, . . . 'what works in cable television news is not an objective analysis of the day's events' but 'a specific point of view on a sizzling-hot topic.' Nicholas Lemann made the same point in a recent New Yorker profile of Bill O'Reilly. Cable, he wrote 'is increasingly a medium of outsize, super-opinionated franchise personalities.'" Michael Kinsley, "The Twilight of Objectivity," *The Washington Post* of March 31, 2006 (www.washingtonpost.com/wp-dyn/content/article/2006/03/30/AR2006033001330.html).

2 For a further elaboration of this argument, see my review of *The News About the News: American Journalism in Peril* by Leonard Downie, Jr. and Robert Kaiser, in *National Review* of April 8, 2002 ("Poses from Posties," vol. LIV, no. 6).

3 "Too Casual to Sit on Press Row?" by Alan Sipress in *The Washington Post* of January 11, 2007 (www.washingtonpost.com/wp-dyn/content/article/2007/01/10/AR2007011002424.html).

4 "A Report to Our Readers" by L. Gordon Crovitz in *The Wall Street Journal* of January 2, 2007 (http://online.wsj.com/article/SB116498997167038202.html).

5 *Ibid.*

Notes

6 See his *Bias: A CBS Insider Exposes How the Media Distort the News* (Washington, DC: Regnery, 2001) and my review of it in *The New Criterion* of February, 2002 ("The charges & countercharges of self-righteous prigs," vol. 20, no. 6).

7 "The latest Pew survey confirms—with lots of numbers—an especially disturbing trend that we've all sensed: People are increasingly picking their media on the basis of partisanship. If you're Republican and conservative, you listen to talk radio and watch the Fox News Channel. If you're liberal and Democratic, you listen to National Public Radio and watch 'The NewsHour With Jim Lehrer.'" Robert Samuelson, "Bull Market for Media Bias" in *The Washington Post* of June 23, 2004 (www.washington post.com/wp-dyn/articles/A62453-2004Jun22.html).

8 "39% See Bias in Reporting on Campaign" by Howard Kurtz in *The Washington Post* of January 12, 2004 (pqasb.pqarchiver.com/washington post/access/523336481.html?dids=523336481:523336481&FMT=ABS& FMTS=ABS:FT&date=Jan+12%2C+2004&author=Howard+Kurtz&pub =The+Washington+Post&edition=&startpage=A.06&desc=39%25+See +Bias+In+Reporting+On+Campaign).

9 See, for example, the 2001 survey by the Kaiser Family Foundation and the Roper Center's *Public Perspective* magazine mentioned by Robert Samuelson in "A Liberal Bias?" in *The Washington Post* of August 29, 2001 (pqasb.pqarchiver.com/washingtonpost/access/78979929.html? dids=78979929:78979929&FMT=ABS&FMTS=ABS:FT&date=Aug+29 %2C+2001&author=Robert+J.+Samuelson&pub=The+Washington+Pos t&edition=&startpage=A.21&desc=A+Liberal+Bias%3F). See also the Dedman survey for MSNBC mentioned below.

10 In an interview on the Hugh Hewitt radio show as cited in 'WashPost Vet: By 25:1, Journalists "Overwhelmingly to the Left,"' MRC "CyberAlert" No. 2277 (vol. 11, no. 164) of September 29, 2006 (www.mrc.org/cyber alerts/2006/cyb20060929.asp#5).

11 See "Journalists dole out cash to politicians (quietly)" by Bill Dedman on MSNBC online from June 25, 2007 (www.msnbc.msn.com/id/ 19113485/).

12 This is the view of Eric Alterman in *What Liberal Media?: The Truth about Bias and News* (New York: Basic Books, 2003).

13 *Ibid.*

14 This was also the view of Sheldon J. Binn, an assistant metropolitan

editor at *The New York Times* for thirty-one years before his retirement in 1988, in a letter published in *The Wall Street Journal* of August 6, 2003: "Responsible news editors have never seen 'objectivity' as their goal. They knew human nature precludes that. But they did strive for 'fairness'—to give both sides a fair shake and let the reader decide."

15 See "Rather Spoke at Democratic Fundraiser," by Howard Kurtz in *The Washington Post* of April 4, 2001 and "Rather Apology Isn't Enough for Some Detractors," by Howard Kurtz in *The Washington Post* of April 5, 2001 (pqasb.pqarchiver.com/washingtonpost/access/70499230.html? dids=70499230:70499230&FMT=ABS&FMTS=ABS:FT&date=Apr+ 4%2C+2001&author=Howard+Kurtz&pub=The+Washington+Post& edition=&startpage=A.01&desc=Rather+Spoke+at+Democratic+Fund raiser) and (pqasb.pqarchiver.com/washingtonpost/access/70532498. html?dids=70532498:70532498&FMT=ABS&FMTS=ABS:FT&date= Apr+5%2C+2001&author=Howard+Kurtz&pub=The+Washington+Post &edition=&startpage=C.02&desc=Rather+Apology+Isn%27t+Enough+ for+Some+Detractors).

16 Howard Kurtz, "Four Syllables, Starts With M, Ends With Uh-Oh" in *The Washington Post* of February 12, 2007 (www.washingtonpost.com/ wp-dyn/content/article/2007/02/11/AR2007021101531.html).

17 See Chapter Six, pp. 106ff.

18 In a column written for the *Salt Lake Tribune* in 2003, as quoted in the Media Research Center "CyberAlert" of August 19, 2003 (www.mrc.org/ cyberalerts/2003/cyb20030819.asp#4). Compare Tom Brokaw's handsome admission to Phil Donahue on the latter's show on MSNBC on July 25, 2002: "I don't think it's a liberal agenda. It happens that journalism will always be spending more time on issues that seem to be liberal to some people; the problem of the downtrodden, the problem of civil rights and human rights, the problem of those people who don't have a place at the table with the powerful" Quoted in "Notable Quotables" of the MRC for August 19, 2002 (www.mrc.org/notablequotables/2002/nq20020819.asp).

19 *Ibid.*

20 For other examples, see my "Cutting Moral Corners" in *The New Criterion* of December, 2004 (vol. XXII, no. 4).

21 See my "Rhetorical recklessness" in *The New Criterion* of October, 2004 (vol. XXII, no. 2).

22 See Chapter Four, p. 82.

Notes

23 For a fuller discussion of this case, see my "New Era in Scandalology" in *The New Criterion* of November, 2006 (vol. XXIV, no. 3).

Chapter Two

1 To an article by Jack Malvern in the edition of December 21, 2006 (www.timesonline.co.uk/article/0,,3-2514037,00.html).

2 Headline to an article by Adam Nagourney in the edition of July 9, 2007 (www.nytimes.com/2007/07/09/us/politics/09voters.html?th&emc=th).

3 Frank Furedi, *Therapy Culture: Cultivating Vulnerability in an Uncertain Age* (London and New York: Routledge, 2004), pp. 24ff.

4 See my article, "The Aristocracy of Feelings," in *The New Criterion* of September, 2002 (vol. XX, no. 1).

5 For a fuller discussion of the cultural transition from heroism to celebrity, see my *Honor: A History* (New York: Encounter Books, 2006).

6 Furedi, pp. 45.

7 See my article, "The postmodern presidential race,' in *The New Criterion* of September, 1996 (vol. xv, no.2).

8 "Perspective on her side, Mrs. Edwards enters fray," by Adam Nagourney and Patrick Healy in *The New York Times* of July 1, 2007 (www.nytimes.com/2007/07/01/us/politics/01edwards.html?th&emc=th).

9 "Bush May Be Out of Chances for a Lasting Domestic Victory,"in *The Washington Post* of June 29, 2007 (www.washingtonpost.com/wp-dyn/content/article/2007/06/28/AR2007062802585.html?hpid=topnews).

10 "Weenie Roast: A Defense of Ann Coulter" by Elspeth Reeve on *The New Republic* online from August 15, 2006 (www.tnr.com/doc.mhtml?i=w060814&s=reeve081506).

11 "Pain does not lead to judgment" in *The Times* of September 27, 2006 (www.timesonline.co.uk/article/0,,6-2376729,00.html).

12 "The Left, Online and Outraged: Liberal Blogger Finds an Outlet and a Community" by David Finkel in *The Washington Post* of April 15, 2006 (www.washingtonpost.com/wp-dyn/content/article/2006/04/14/AR2006041401648.html).

13 See, for example, Ted Gup, "America's Secret Obsession" in *The Washington Post* of June 10, 2007 (www.washingtonpost.com/wp-dyn/content/article/2007/06/08/AR2007060802496.html).

Chapter Three

1 Comic strip drawn by Bill Griffith (June 25, 2007). Mr. Griffith also makes frequent use for satirical purposes of the media trope of the Bush-Cheney administration's alleged delusions or detachment from reality, as for example in "Bubble Trouble" of September 6, 2007.

2 See note 11 in Chapter One.

3 Quoted in "Notable Quotables" of the Media Research Center, July 2, 2007 (www.mrc.org/notablequotables/2007/nq20070702.asp).

4 Quoted in MRC "CyberAlert" of June 26, 2007 (www.mrc.org/cyberalerts/2007/cyb20070626.asp#5).

5 "Bush like Hitler, says first Muslim in Congress," by Toby Harnden in the London *Sunday Telegraph* of July 15, 2007 (www.telegraph.co.uk/news/main.jhtml?xml=/news/2007/07/14/wbush114.xml).

6 As TRB, "At Long Last," in *The New Republic* of October 2, 2006. (www.tnr.com/doc.mhtml?i=20061002&s=trb100206).

7 *American Theocracy: The Peril and Politics of Radical Religion, Oil, and Borrowed Money in the 21st Century* (New York: Viking, 2006).

8 Edition of February 25, 2007.

9. "Without a Doubt" in *The New York Times* Magazine of October 17, 2004 (select.nytimes.com/search/restricted/article?res=F30F1EF93A5F0 C748DDDA90994DC404482#).

10 A Google search of "reality-based community" in September 2007 turned up "about" 726,000 citations. In *The New York Times* see "Bush's Blinkers" by Bob Herbert, October 22, 2004 (select.nytimes.com/search/restricted/article?res=F20D1EFD355E0C718EDDA90994DC404482); "Bono's New Casualty: 'Private Ryan,'" by Frank Rich, November 21, 2004 (select.nytimes.com/search/restricted/article?res=F40D15FD395B0C72 8EDDA80994DC404482); "Kansas on my mind" by Paul Krugman, February 25, 2005 (select.nytimes.com/search/restricted/article?res=FA0 C12F63C590C768EDDAB0894DD404482); "Haunted by Hesitation" by Maureen Dowd, September 7, 2005 (select.nytimes.com/search/restricted/article?res=FA0C12F63C590C768EDDAB0894DD404482); among many others.

11 New York: Simon & Schuster, 2006.

12 "President Bush's Reality" in *The New York Times* of September 12,

Notes

2006 (www.nytimes.com/2006/09/12/opinion/12tue1.html?th&emc=th). The *Times's* editorial writers liked this idea of Mr. Bush's detachment from reality so much that it returned to it on many subsequent occasions over the next several months, and they are still returning to it as I write. See, for example,"Iraq and the Facts of Life" of November 29, 2006 (www.nytimes.com/2006/11/29/opinion/29wed1.html?th&emc=th), "Ranting at Reality" of April 26, 2007 (www.nytimes.com/2007/04/26/opinion/26thu2.html?th&emc=th), "Mr Bush Alone" of May 11, 2007 (www.nytimes.com/2007/05/11/opinion/11fri1.html?th&emc=th), "War Without End" of May 27, 2007 (www.nytimes.com/2007/05/27/opinion/27sun1.html?th&emc=th), and "No Progress Report" of July 13, 2007 (www.nytimes.com/2007/07/13/opinion/13fri1.html?th&emc=th).

13 *Ibid.*

14 For a further discussion of the place of this event in the media's iconography of the Iraq war, see my "Cheap Laughs" in *The New Criterion* of June, 2006 (vol. XXIV, no. 10).

15 See, for instance, 'Saddam's Terror Training Camps' by Stephen F. Hayes in *The Weekly Standard* of January 16, 2006 (vol. XI, no. 17), and the same author's "Saddam's Philippines Terror Connection and other revelations from the Iraqi files" in *The Weekly Standard* of March 27, 2006 (vol. XI, no. 26).

16 "Has he Started Talking to the Walls?" in *The New York Times* of December 3, 2006 (select.nytimes.com/2006/12/03/opinion/03rich.html?).

17 New York: Penguin Press, 2006. For an account of Mr. Rich's own lapses from the strictest regard for veracity, see "Frank Rich's Truthiness" by Christopher Hitchens in *The Claremont Review of Books*, Winter 2006–07 (vol. VII, no. 1, pp 10-12). For a fuller discussion of Mr. Rich's specious reasoning, see my "Delusions of 'Reality'" in *The New Criterion* of January, 2007 (vol. XXV, no. 5).

18 See, for example, Sharon Begley, "The Truths We Want to Deny" in *Newsweek* of May 21, 2007 (www.msnbc.msn.com/id/18629197/site/newsweek/page/0/). Shankar Vedantam, "Bush: Naturally, Never Wrong" in *The Washington Post* of July 9, 2007 (www.washingtonpost.com/wp-dyn/content/article/2007/07/08/AR2007070800742.html).

19 "Daffy Does Doom" in *The New York Times* of January 27, 2007 (select.nytimes.com/2007/01/27/opinion/27dowd.html?th&emc=th).

20 "A Vice President Without Borders, Bordering on Lunacy" in" *The*

New York Times of June 24, 2007 (select.nytimes.com/2007/06/24/opinion/ 24dowd.html?th&emc=th).

21 See Chapter One, pp 20–21.

22 "Lies, Sighs and Politics" in *The New York Times* of June 8, 2007 (select.nytimes.com/2007/06/08/opinion/08krugman.html?th&emc=th).

23 "Trust and Betrayal" in *The New York Times* of May 28, 2007 (select. nytimes.com/2007/05/28/opinion/28krugman.html?th&emc=th).

24 "Bush vs. Reality" in *The Washington Post* of September 21, 2006 (www.washingtonpost.com/wp-dyn/content/blog/2006/09/21/BL2006 092100764.html). This is a favorite idea of this columnist. See also, for example, his "The Delusional Duo" of November 29, 2006: "Who's more delusional about Iraq: President Bush or Iraqi Prime Minister Nouri al-Maliki?"

25 *The Spirit of Terrorism: Requiem for the Twin Towers* (2002); revised edition (London and New York: Verso, 2003).

26 "Don't Fear the A-Word" in *The Washington Post* of May 22, 2007 (www.washingtonpost.com/wp-dyn/content/article/2007/05/21/ AR2007052101468.html).

27 See "How's this for Satire" by Richard Cohen, in *The Washington Post* of March 14, 2006 (www.washingtonpost.com/wp-dyn/content/article/ 2006/03/13/AR2006031301484.html).

Chapter Four

1 "I hate e-mail," in *The Times* of May 5, 2007 (www.entertainment. timesonline.co.uk/tol/arts_and_entertainment/books/article1747024.ece).

2 By, for instance, Jeff Randall in "Rediscovering the Lost Art of Elegant Abuse" in the *Daily Telegraph* of June 8, 2007 (www.telegraph.co.uk/ opinion/main.jhtml?xml=/opinion/2007/06/08/do0801.xml).

3 "In Iowa Yard, Biden Talks (and Talks) About Experience" by Jeff Zeleny in *The New York Times* of July 7, 2007 (www.nytimes.com/2007/ 07/07/us/politics/07biden.html?ex=1189224000&en=54bdca398d51ab96 &ei=5070).

4 *Baseball Between the Numbers* edited by Jonah Keri. (New York: Basic Books, 2006).

5 *The Gospel of Food* by Barry Glassner (New York: Ecco Books, 2007).

Notes

6 See *The Bell Curve: Intelligence and Class Structure in American Life* (New York: Free Press, 1994, 1996), p. 25 ff. "The twentieth century dawned on a world segregated into social classes defined in terms of money, power, and status. The ancient lines of separation based on hereditary rank were being erased, replaced by a more complicated set of overlapping lines. . . . Our thesis is that the twentieth century has continued the transformation, so that the twenty-first will open on a world in which cognitive ability is the decisive dividing force. The shift is more subtle than the previous one but more momentous. Social class remains the vehicle of social life, but intelligence now pulls the train."

7 "The Politics of the Lonely Crowd: Protest Movements Get Personal" in spiked-online.com from 9 March 2004 (www.spiked-online.com/Articles/0000000CA449.htm).

8 See Chapter One, p 25.

9 "Who's the Man?" in *The New York Times Book Review* of March 19, 2006 (www.nytimes.com/2006/03/19/books/review/19kirn.html).

10 For a fuller discussion of this election and the partisan involvement in it of *The Washington Post*, see my article, "Biased Sensationalism," in *The New Criterion* of December, 2006 (vol. XXIV, no, 3).

11 "New Media a Weapon in New World of Politics," in *The Washington Post* of October 6, 2006 (www.washingtonpost.com/wp-dyn/content/article/2006/10/05/AR2006100501811.html).

12 From *The Guardian* of February 3, 2004, quoted by Kevin Cullen in "Broadcast Blues" in *The Boston Globe* of February 15, 2004 (www.boston.com/news/globe/ideas/articles/2004/02/15/broadcast_blues?mode=PF).

Chapter Five

1 "Who Really 'Owns' Sept. 11?" in *The Washington Post* of March 9, 2004 (www.washingtonpost.com/wp-dyn/articles/A41694-2004Mar8.html).The emphasis is mine.

2 "Pakistan Government Intervenes in Rushdie Row" by Peter Foster in the *Daily Telegraph* of June 19, 2007 (www.telegraph.co.uk/news/main.jhtml?xml=/news/2007/06/19/wrushdie119.xml).

3 See "655,000 Iraqi Civilians Dead. Who Are the Terrorists?"' in MRC "CyberAlert" No. 2413 (vol. XII, no. 86) of May 22, 2007 (www.mrc.org/cyberalerts/2007/cyb20070522.asp#1).

4 See the Media Research Center "CyberAlert" number 2274 (Volume xi, no. 160) of September 25, 2006 (www.mrc.org/cyberalerts/2006/ cyb20060925.asp#6).

5 For a list of examples, see John McCandlish Phillips in "When Columnists Cry 'Jihad'" in *The Washington Post* of May 4, 2005 (www.washington post.com/wp-dyn/content/article/2005/05/03/AR2005050301277.html).

6 On the ABC television program "The View" of September 12, 2006, as recorded by the Media Research Center (www.mrc.org/cyberalerts/ 2006/cyb20060913.asp#3).

7 As recorded by the Media Research Center (www.mrc.org/cyber alerts/2006/cyb20060914.asp#1).

8 See "Turner Takes Credit for Ending Cold War, Spouts Other Silliness" in MRC "CyberAlert" No. 2273 (vol. XI, no. 159) of September 22, 2006 (www.mrc.org/cyberalerts/2006/cyb20060922.asp#1).

9 "Presidents Spar Over Iran's Aims and US Power" by Jim Rutenberg and Helene Cooper in *The New York Times* of September 20, 2006 (www.nytimes.com/2006/09/20/world/middleeast/20prexy.html?th& emc=th).

10 See James Fallows, *Breaking the News, How the Media Undermine American Democracy* (New York: Vintage Books, 1997), pp. 10–16.

11 "Letter from Bill Keller on *The Times*'s Banking Records Report" in *The New York Times* of June 25, 2006 (www.nytimes.com/2006/06/25/ business/media/25keller-letter.html).

12 "Pentagon Pursues Leak of Anti-Iraq Plan" in *The New York Times* of July 20, 2002.

13 See Media Research Center "CyberAlert" of July 22, 2003 (www.mrc. org/cyberalerts/2003/cyb20030722.asp).

14 See "ABC Alerts Ayatollahs of CIA's 'Secret' 'Hidden War' Against Iran" by Scott Whitlock of the Media Research Center's "Newsbusters" of May 23, 2007 (newsbusters.org/node/12954).

15 February 12, 2007, as recorded in "Cafferty Draws Moral Equivalence Between Iran and United States," MRC "CyberAlert" No. 2357 (vol. XII, no 27) of February 13, 2007 (www.mrc.org/cyberalerts/2007/cyb2007 0213.asp#1).

Notes

Chapter Six

1 *Daily Telegraph* of July 10, 2007 (www.telegraph.co.uk/news/main. jhtml?xml=/news/2007/07/10/nmadonna110.xml).

2 "A Blog That Made It Big" in *The Washington Post* of July 9, 2007 (www.washingtonpost.com/wp-dyn/content/article/2007/07/08/ AR2007070801213.html).

3 See Chapter Three, p. 46.

4 *The Importance of Being Famous: Behind the Scenes of the Celebrity-Industrial Complex* by Maureen Orth (New York: Henry Holt, 2007). Quoted in *The Washington Post* review, "All that Glitters," by Martha Sherrill, May 2, 2004 (www.washingtonpost.com/wp-dyn/articles/ A54844-2004Apr29.html).

5 "Rags to Riches: The Trashy Magazine With a Posh Audience" by Emma Chastain on *The New Republic* online from July 15, 2004 (www.tnr.com/doc.mhtml?i=online&s=chastain071504).

6 "This Idiocy is all John Lennon's Fault" by Michael Henderson in *Daily Telegraph* of July 7, 2007 (www.telegraph.co.uk/opinion/main.jhtml? xml=/opinion/2007/07/07/do0705.xml).

7 *Ibid.*

8 Alessandra Stanley, "Sounding the Global-Warming Alarm Without Upsetting the Fans" in *The New York Times* of July 9, 2007 (www.nytimes. com/2007/07/09/arts/television/09watc.html?th&emc=th).

9 "Why Live Earth was a Dead Loss" by Neil McCormick in the *Daily Telegraph* of July 10, 2007 (www.telegraph.co.uk/arts/main.jhtml?xml= /arts/2007/07/10/bmliveearth1.xml).

10 See Chapter Five, p. 91.

11 "Critic's Notebook: Tony Bennett Turns 80, A Rock of Reassurance" by Stephen Holden in *The New York Times* of August 2, 2006 (select.nytimes.com/search/restricted/article?res=F30E1FFF3B5B0C718 CDDA10894DE40448).

12 See Chapter Three, pp. 52–54.

Index

Index

Index

Index

MEDIA MADNESS has been set in Adobe Systems' Warnock Pro, an OpenType font designed in 1997 by Robert Slimbach. Named for John Warnock, one of Adobe's co-founders, the roman was originally intended for its namesake's personal use, but was later developed into a comprehensive family of types. Although the type is based firmly in Slimbach's calligraphic work, the completed family makes abundant use of the refinements attainable via digitization. With its range of optical sizes, Warnock Pro is elegant in display settings, warm and readable at text sizes – a classical design with contemporary adaptability.

SERIES DESIGN BY CARL W. SCARBROUGH